Data Science and Analytics Essentials

The Revolution of Decision-Making: Leveraging Data in the Digital Age

Daniel Richards

Table of Contents

INTRODUCTION

In an era where information is the new currency, data science and analytics have emerged as pivotal disciplines driving the modern revolution in decision-making. "Data Science and Analytics Essentials: The Revolution of Decision-Making: Leveraging Data in the Digital Age" is designed to serve as a comprehensive guide for professionals, students, and enthusiasts eager to harness the power of data to make informed, strategic decisions.

The digital age has unleashed an unprecedented explosion of data, transforming how organizations operate and compete. From healthcare and finance to marketing and transportation, data-driven insights are reshaping industries and redefining the boundaries of what is possible. This book delves into the core principles and practices that underpin the field of data science, offering readers a clear roadmap to navigate the complexities of data collection, preparation, analysis, and interpretation.

Through a blend of theoretical foundations and practical applications, we will explore the essential tools, techniques, and methodologies that data scientists and analysts employ to extract meaningful patterns and insights from vast datasets. Readers will gain an understanding of both the statistical and computational aspects of the field, equipping them with the knowledge to tackle real-world challenges.

As we embark on this journey, we will also consider the ethical implications and responsibilities that come with wielding powerful data-driven tools. By the end of this book, you will be well-prepared to leverage data in ways that drive innovation, efficiency, and success in the digital age. Welcome to the revolution of decision-making.

CHAPTER I

Data Science and Analytics

Definition and Importance

One of the fields that will change society the most in the twenty-first century is data science, which significantly impacts everything from business and healthcare to government and education. Fundamentally, data science is an interdisciplinary area that draws knowledge and insights from structured and unstructured data using scientific procedures, systems, algorithms, and methods. It integrates concepts from computer science, statistics, and domain-specific expertise to analyze and comprehend large, complex data sets. This process eventually promotes innovation and well-informed decision-making.

The term "data science" encompasses several essential elements. Data collection, or compiling information from multiple sources, is the first step. These sources can be anything from social media posts, sensor data from Internet of Things devices, transactional data from businesses to massive databases produced by scientific studies. Data processing and cleansing is the following phase in the data science pipeline. Raw data frequently needs extensive preparation to make it appropriate for analysis because it is disorganized and incomplete. In this step, errors are fixed, missing values are handled, and data formats are normalized.

Data scientists use various analytical techniques to find patterns and relationships in the prepared data. The data must be described and summarized using statistical methods, and future trends and behaviors must be predicted using machine learning algorithms. Additionally, visualization tools are essential to data science because they make complex data more accessible to view and comprehend. The conclusions drawn from these assessments are subsequently applied to strategy development, process optimization, and decision-making.

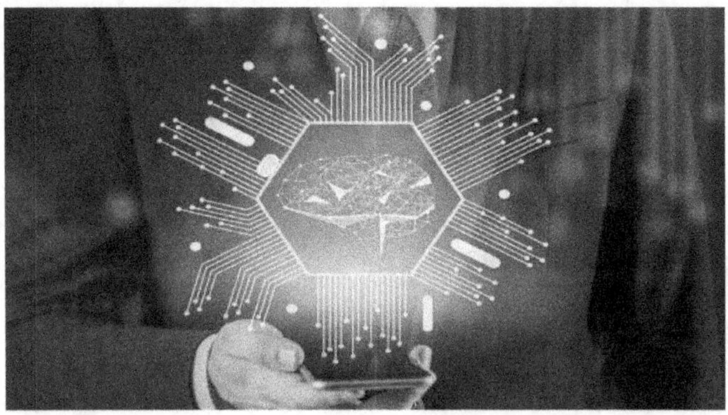

In today's data-driven society, data science is vital and cannot be emphasized enough. The rapid expansion of data, also known as "big data," has made it imperative to have reliable techniques for organizing and interpreting this data. This requirement is fulfilled by data science, which offers the methods and tools necessary to transform enormous volumes of data into valuable insights. This can entail expanding a company's consumer base, finding new markets to enter, and increasing operational effectiveness. Data science in healthcare makes it possible to identify diseases early and create individualized treatment options. It facilitates the creation of data-driven policies and assesses their effects on public policy.

Improving decision-making processes is one of data science's most important contributions. Conventional decision-making frequently depended on experience and intuition. These components are still important, but data-driven insights are increasingly complementing and, in many cases, surpassing them. Organizations can make more precise, fact-based decisions because of the capacity to analyze enormous volumes of data and identify significant trends. Several industries have seen a shift in decision-making toward data-driven approaches.

For example, data science has transformed marketing methods in the commercial world. Businesses can now customize their products and services to match individual demands by analyzing client data to understand preferences and habits. Companies can acquire an edge using predictive analytics to foresee consumer requests and market trends. This is especially crucial in today's competitive market, where making quick, well-informed decisions is essential to remaining one step ahead.

Data science has also been highly beneficial to the healthcare industry. Precision medicine has advanced due to its capacity to analyze massive datasets from genetic data, electronic health records, and clinical trials. By finding patterns in patient data, healthcare practitioners can lower healthcare expenses, enhance patient outcomes, and create more effective treatment regimens. Predictive analytics can also aid in early disease detection and prevention, significantly improving public health.

In the field of public policy, data science gives decision-makers the means to examine social and economic data, allowing them to create policies that more effectively meet the populace's requirements. For instance, analyzing data on economic indicators, education levels, and crime rates can help determine regions needing assistance and allocate resources more effectively. Additionally, data science can be beneficial in assessing the effects of policies, enabling ongoing modification and advancement.

Environmental science is another field where data science is significantly influencing it. Scientists can learn more about climate change and its effects by examining data from environmental sensors, climate models, and satellite photos. Access to this information is crucial for making educated judgments about resource management and conservation initiatives and formulating measures to mitigate climate change.

Incorporating data science into contemporary decision-making procedures also presents new duties and obstacles. Since the ability to analyze and understand data might be abused, ethical data use is an essential factor to consider. Concerns, including bias, security, and data privacy, must be appropriately handled to guarantee that data science procedures are equitable and just. Organizations need robust data governance structures to safeguard sensitive data and ensure adherence to laws like the California Consumer Privacy Act (CCPA) and the General Data Protection Regulation (GDPR).

Furthermore, data science is a constantly changing subject fueled by data availability and technological breakthroughs. Emerging technologies like machine learning, quantum computing, and artificial intelligence (AI) are pushing the limits of data analysis. These developments strengthen data science's potential and create new avenues for creativity and problem-solving.

To sum up, data science is an exciting and potent field vital to contemporary decision-making. Organizations can drive innovation in various industries, obtain more profound insights, and make better decisions using data. In the digital age, analyzing and comprehending data is becoming increasingly important, and data science will only become more and more influential as technology develops and the amount of data grows. But with this authority also comes the need to utilize data sensibly and ethically, ensuring that data science's advantages are achieved while upholding public confidence and safeguarding individual privacy. Data science will play an increasingly more important part in determining how decisions are made in the future, making it a vital tool in the digital age.

Historical Context

Thanks to major turning points and technical breakthroughs that have revolutionized data collection, processing, and analysis, data science and analytics fields have experienced a fantastic evolution. Understanding the historical background of this development is essential to understanding how data science has integrated itself into contemporary innovation and decision-making.

Data science originates in the early stages of data analysis and statistics. Mathematicians like Thomas Bayes and Carl Friedrich Gauss established the basis in the 18th century with ideas like the Gaussian distribution and the Bayes theorem. These pioneering efforts laid the statistical foundations of many aspects of contemporary data science. More advanced statistical methods began to appear in the 19th century. For example, industry pioneers Karl Pearson and Francis Galton developed regression analysis and correlation, which are still used today.

Data science and analytics development saw a dramatic shift in the 20th century. The ability to process data was transformed by the introduction of computers in the middle of the 20th century. One of the first general-purpose computers, the Electronic Numerical Integrator and Computer (ENIAC), was created in 1946 and made data computation more effective. During this time, critical theoretical underpinnings were also established. For example, 1948, Claude Shannon developed information theory, which offered a mathematical framework for comprehending data transmission and storage.

Significant developments were made in the 1960s and 1970s with the creation of databases and data management systems. Edgar F. Codd's 1970 presentation of the relational database model marked a revolutionary turning point. Thanks to this paradigm, large datasets could be efficiently organized and retrieved, which laid the groundwork for contemporary database management systems (DBMS) like Oracle and MySQL. Developed in the 1970s, Structured Query Language (SQL) greatly improved data handling capabilities by becoming the standard language for maintaining and querying relational databases.

Business intelligence and data warehousing development occurred in the 1980s and 1990s. Businesses started to realize how valuable it was to combine data from several sources into centralized repositories called data warehouses. Consolidation made it possible to analyze and report data more thoroughly. Online Analytical Processing (OLAP) was developed during this period, enabling multidimensional data processing and sophisticated analytical queries. With the rise in popularity of business intelligence tools like SAS and Microsoft Excel, firms were able to conclude their data better.

The internet era, which began in the late 1990s and early 2000s, significantly boosted the amount and variety of data generated. Web analytics became popular during this time, and the significance of monitoring user behavior online was realized. Companies such as Google pioneered web analytics technologies, which offer insights into website traffic, user interactions, and the efficacy of online marketing. Due to the internet's data explosion, more sophisticated data processing and storage technologies were required.

A pivotal point in data science and analytics development was the emergence of big data in the mid-2000s. The phrase "big data" describes datasets that are too enormous, too complicated, or change too quickly for conventional data processing techniques to handle. Extensive data management and analysis tools were developed by companies such as Google and Yahoo! Large datasets could be processed across computer clusters in a distributed manner thanks to Google's MapReduce framework, first released in 2004. This breakthrough allowed the Hadoop ecosystem to grow, an open-source framework now the mainstay of big data processing.

The amount of data generated increased even more in the late 2000s and early 2010s with the emergence of social media platforms. Social media sites like Facebook, Twitter, and LinkedIn made new sources of unstructured data, such as text, photos, and videos, available. Sentiment analysis and natural language processing (NLP) techniques became popular in this era, enabling businesses to examine and comprehend user thoughts and sentiments expressed on social media. Gaining knowledge from unstructured data became increasingly crucial.

Another wave of data collection and analysis emerged in the 2010s due to the widespread use of mobile devices and the Internet of Things (IoT). Vast volumes of real-time data are constantly being produced by Internet of Things (IoT) devices, including wearables, smart appliances, and intelligent sensors. New data processing and storage methods were needed due to this data inflow. Technologies like Apache Spark and Kafka were developed to handle real-time data streams and do real-time analytics. This allowed enterprises to make decisions more quickly and intelligently.

One of the most significant developments in recent years has been the growth of artificial intelligence (AI) and machine learning. Data science relies heavily on machine learning techniques, letting computers learn from data and forecast future events. Advances in image identification, natural language processing, and autonomous systems have resulted from the 2010s' emergence of deep learning and the revival of neural networks. Businesses like Google, Facebook, and Amazon have used these technologies to develop cutting-edge goods and services, such as virtual assistants and recommendation algorithms.

The democratization of data science tools and platforms is another indicator of the continuous development of data science and analytics. A more comprehensive range of people now have access to advanced data science tools because of the growth of open-source software and cloud computing. Data scientists now depend heavily on platforms like Jupyter, TensorFlow, and PyTorch, making it simple to create and implement machine learning models. Cloud services that offer scalable infrastructure for data processing, analytics, and storage, such as Microsoft Azure, Google Cloud Platform (GCP), and Amazon Web Services (AWS), allow businesses of all sizes to take advantage of data science.

Technology breakthroughs and an increasing understanding of the significance of data-driven decision-making have fueled the development of data science and analytics. After adopting data science as a strategic advantage, businesses in various sectors have invested in data infrastructure, talent, and culture. Businesses driven by data, like Netflix, Uber, and Airbnb, have upended conventional business models using data to tailor experiences and streamline processes. Because of the increased need for qualified data scientists, academic institutions and professional associations have started offering data science degrees and certifications.

In summary, significant turning points and technical developments that have revolutionized data collection, processing, and analysis have influenced the development of data science and analytics. Data science has developed into a vital instrument for contemporary innovation and decision-making, from the early days of statistical analysis to the era of big data, machine learning, and artificial intelligence. The area of data science will undoubtedly continue to develop, leading to discoveries and influencing the direction of technology and society, as long as data volume and complexity continue to rise. We can better recognize the significant influence of data science and look forward to its exciting future advancements when we know this historical background.

The Digital Age and Data Explosion

The advent of the Digital Age has led to an unparalleled period of data generation, commonly known as the "data explosion." This phenomenon has completely changed how data is generated, gathered, and evaluated. It is fueled by the increasing use of digital technology and the Internet. This digital change has led directly to the growth of big data, which significantly impacts individuals, governments, and corporations.

Datasets that are too massive, too complicated, or change too quickly for conventional data processing techniques are referred to as big data. The three V's—volume, velocity, and variety—are the three essential components of big data. The terms volume, velocity, and variety all relate to the sheer amount of data generated, the speed at which it is produced and processed, and the various forms of data, such as structured, unstructured, and semi-structured data.

The digital age began with the development of the Internet in the late 20th century, which paved the way for the explosion of data. At first, the Internet served as a storehouse for basic web pages and text-based content. But as technology advanced quickly, more sophisticated content—such as pictures, movies, and interactive applications—could soon be produced. Data generation was significantly expedited in the mid-2000s with the emergence of social media platforms. Social media sites like Facebook, Instagram, and Twitter have emerged as essential providers of user-generated content, generating enormous volumes of data daily. People started exchanging ideas, pictures, videos, and conversations, resulting in a rich and varied collection of unstructured data.

The data explosion has also been significantly influenced by mobile technology. Thanks to the widespread use of smartphones and other mobile devices, people may now more easily access the Internet and create data on the road. Mobile apps add to the expanding data by tracking user activity, preferences, and locations. Furthermore, incorporating sensors into these gadgets has made it possible to gather real-time data on various activities, such as social interactions, navigation, and health and fitness.

The Internet of Things (IoT) further exacerbated the data explosion. The Internet of Things (IoT) is a network of gadgets that can communicate and share data. These gadgets range from industrial sensors and driverless cars to wearable fitness trackers and intelligent household appliances. IoT devices generate vast amounts of continuous data that offer real-time insights into various aspects of everyday living and industrial activities. Smart meters monitor energy consumption, while connected cars provide information on driving behavior and efficiency.

Digital transformation has also transformed traditional industries, producing enormous volumes of data. Large patient data repositories have been produced in the healthcare industry as a result of the digitalization of medical records and the application of cutting-edge diagnostic techniques. Research, tailored therapy, and better healthcare outcomes all benefit greatly from this data. Comparably, digital transactions, online banking, and electronic trading create massive datasets in the financial sector that are examined for customer insights, risk mitigation, and fraud detection.

The data explosion has been largely attributed to the growth of e-commerce. Online merchants gather information about consumer behavior, tastes, and buying habits to improve customer satisfaction and marketing tactics. Platforms such as Amazon and Alibaba analyze large volumes of transaction data to manage inventories, forecast trends, and provide product recommendations. As a result of this data-driven strategy, the retail industry has changed, becoming more competitive and customer-focused.

Digital transformation's effects also impact the public sector on data generation. Governments worldwide are using big data to enhance public services and policymaking. By analyzing data from multiple sources, such as social media, sensors, and public records, governments may improve public safety, better understand their citizens' needs and preferences, and allocate resources more efficiently. Intelligent city efforts, for instance, make better use of data from IoT devices to control traffic, save energy use, and enhance urban planning.

New technologies and procedures have had to be developed to properly handle and evaluate the massive amount of data that the digital age has produced. Big data's magnitude and complexity make traditional data processing methods and technologies ineffective. As a result, sophisticated data processing frameworks such as Apache Hadoop and Apache Spark have surfaced, facilitating the distributed processing of massive datasets among computer clusters. These frameworks, which offer the processing power required to glean insightful information from enormous datasets, have emerged as the mainstay of big data analytics.

One cannot stress the importance of cloud computing in extensive data management. Cloud platforms such as Amazon Web Services (AWS), Microsoft Azure, and Google Cloud offer scalable infrastructure and services for processing, storing, and analyzing large amounts of data. By providing adaptable and affordable solutions, these platforms enable businesses to manage massive data volumes without making costly on-premises hardware purchases. Data-driven decision-making is made more accessible for organizations by the ability to run sophisticated queries and analytics on their data using cloud-based data warehouses like Google BigQuery and Amazon Redshift.

Using artificial intelligence (AI) and machine learning has also proven essential to maximizing the potential of extensive data. Large datasets can be analyzed using machine learning algorithms, which can then be used to find patterns, anticipate outcomes, and automate decision-making. AI-driven tools and applications are revolutionizing several industries, including marketing, finance, healthcare, and transportation. For example, AI-driven recommendation systems in e-commerce increase customer engagement and revenue, while predictive analytics in healthcare can detect disease outbreaks.

Big data has many advantages, but the digital era presents difficulties and worries. Data privacy and security are critical concerns since there is a greater chance of data breaches and misuse due to the massive amount of sensitive and personal data being collected. For businesses handling large amounts of data, ensuring compliance with data protection laws like the California Consumer Privacy Act (CCPA) and the General Data Protection Regulation (GDPR) is essential. It is also necessary to carefully evaluate the ethical implications of data gathering and processing to prevent biases and guarantee fairness.

The emergence of the digital age and the resulting surge in data has completely changed how data is created, gathered, and examined. The growth of digital technology and the Internet has led to the rise of big data, bringing out new opportunities and difficulties for individuals, governments, and organizations. Extensive data analysis and utilization skills are now essential for fostering innovation, better decision-making, and raising the standard of living. The influence of digital transformation on data generation will only increase as technology develops, necessitating the creation of reliable tools, processes, and moral frameworks to manage and use this priceless resource properly.

CHAPTER II

Understanding Data

Types of Data

Studying data science and analytics requires a fundamental understanding of data in all its forms. Three primary categories of data exist: semi-structured, unstructured, and structured. Data is the foundation from which insights are derived. Each data type's features, sources, and analytic techniques affect how it is applied in decision-making procedures. Furthermore, data can be obtained from external sources or within an organization, each with pros and cons.

The most accessible form of data to handle and evaluate is structured data. It is typically kept in databases in a tabular format with rows and columns that clearly describe different data fields and their values. It is incredibly well-organized and highly searchable. Transaction logs, inventory logs, and customer databases are a few structured data types. Business programs, including customer relationship management (CRM), enterprise resource planning (ERP), and finance software, are familiar structured data sources. Structured data is quickly evaluated and queried using structured query language (SQL) and conventional database management systems due to its orderly form.

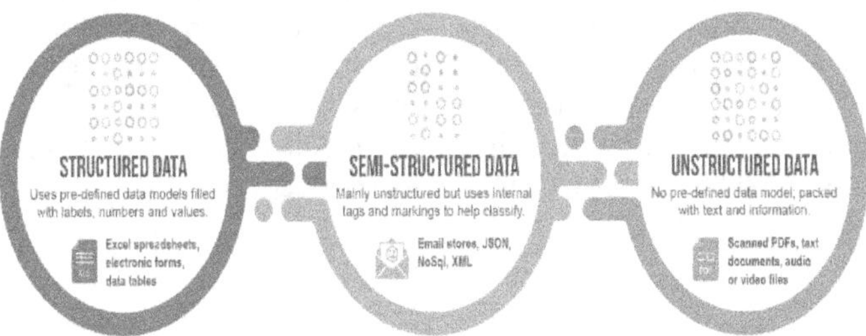

On the other hand, unstructured data lacks a predetermined structure or format. Since this kind of data fits poorly into tables, it is more difficult to analyze it. Text documents, emails, posts on social media, photos, videos, audio files, and other multimedia information are examples of unstructured data. Unstructured data is a valuable source of insights due to its sheer amount and variety, but its analysis calls for specialized tools and methods. To glean patterns and meaning from unstructured data, machine learning techniques and natural language processing (NLP) are frequently utilized. Sentiment analysis, for instance, can be used to determine the consensus from posts on social media, while image recognition algorithms can examine the visual content of images and videos.

Between structured and unstructured data is semi-structured data. Even while it doesn't follow the strict structure of standard databases, it has specific organizational characteristics that facilitate analysis compared to entirely unstructured data. HTML websites, JSON documents, and XML files are semi-structured data examples. These data formats frequently have markers or tags to distinguish between various data items, which makes parsing and organization easier. Semi-structured data is often present in data interchange formats between multiple systems, online applications, and APIs. Semi-structured data is managed and analyzed using tools like NoSQL databases and data integration platforms, which makes it possible to create more adaptable and scalable data solutions.

Internal and external sources can be used to classify data sources broadly. Information created by an organization's activities and transactions is included in internal data from within the company. This information is pertinent to the organization's decision-making procedures and is frequently easily accessible. Some internal data sources are sales records, personnel data, production indicators, and customer contacts. Internal data is essential since it offers precise company operations and performance perspectives. Organizations can find inefficiencies, streamline procedures, and raise performance levels by evaluating internal data.

On the other hand, external data originates from sources outside the company. This kind of information can strengthen and further contextualize the insights obtained from internal data. Market research studies, industry statistics, news stories, social media feeds, and publicly accessible datasets from governmental and other organizations are examples of external data sources. Organizations can discover new opportunities, measure their performance against competitors, and comprehend market trends using external data. For example, a business could estimate product demand using external economic data or adjust its marketing plans based on social media trend analysis.

Integrating internal and external data is a potent strategy that helps businesses obtain a complete picture of their surroundings and make better decisions. However, combining various data sources comes with a number of difficulties. The formats, structures, and quality levels of data from multiple sources can differ, necessitating preprocessing and standardization. When working with internal and external data, it's also essential to carefully manage data security, privacy, and compliance concerns.

Combining and analyzing data from many sources is now more straightforward, thanks to data integration platforms and technology developments. In a centralized location, massive amounts of organized, semi-structured, and unstructured data are frequently kept in warehouses and lakes. While data lakes are made to manage enormous volumes of raw data in their native format, making them appropriate for semi-structured and unstructured data, data warehouses are usually geared for query performance and storing structured data. With the aid of these platforms, businesses can carry out sophisticated analytics and get knowledge from a comprehensive picture of their data environment.

Another crucial component of managing various data sources and types is data governance. Regardless of the form or source, reliable, consistent, and secure data is guaranteed by effective data governance. It entails defining data standards, allocating duties for data stewardship, and creating rules and processes for data management. With the support of a strong data governance structure, organizations can uphold data quality, adhere to legal requirements, and foster confidence in their data-driven decision-making processes.

The emergence of big data and sophisticated analytics has emphasized the significance of comprehending and handling various data types even more. Thanks to big data technologies like Hadoop and Spark, structured, unstructured, and semi-structured data may all be processed and analyzed using large datasets. These technologies open new avenues for insights and creativity by offering the processing capacity and scalability required to handle significant data volume, velocity, and variety.

Artificial intelligence (AI) and machine learning have transformed the examination of many kinds of data. Without explicit programming, machine learning algorithms can autonomously learn from data, spot patterns, and make predictions. Artificial intelligence (AI) methods, including deep learning, have effectively analyzed unstructured data, such as photos, videos, and text in natural language. These developments have raised the potential of data science, allowing for more automated and sophisticated analysis of various kinds of data.

To sum up, studying data science and analytics requires a fundamental grasp of the many forms of data—structured, unstructured, and semi-structured—as well as the sources of that data—internal and external. Because of its well-organized nature, structured data is simple to handle and evaluate, but unstructured data is complex and full of information, requiring sophisticated tools and methods. Finding a middle ground, semi-structured data provides a certain amount of structure without the inflexibility of structured data. While external data adds context and improves decision-making, internal data delivers clear insights into an organization's activities. By integrating different data sources and assisting with data governance and technological improvements, companies may fully utilize their data, fostering innovation and well-informed decision-making in the digital age. Success in the data-driven world will depend increasingly on your ability to comprehend and handle the various forms of data as it grows in volume and complexity.

Data Collection Methods

Data gathering is a critical component of data science, which serves as the foundation for all analyses, insights, and decision-making. There are numerous approaches to gathering data, and each is appropriate for a particular research topic, set of goals, and setting. These techniques span from more contemporary methods like web scraping and data collection from Internet of Things (IoT) devices and sensors to more conventional ways like surveys, experiments, and observational studies. It is essential to comprehend these techniques and how they are used to make sound data-driven decisions.

Surveys are among the most popular and adaptable ways to gather data. They entail interviewing or using questionnaires to collect information from people directly. There are other ways to conduct surveys, such as in-person, over the phone, or online. They are accommodating for gathering information on demographics, attitudes, opinions, and habits. A survey's design is essential to its effectiveness; its questions must be impartial, understandable, and pertinent to the study's goals. One of the benefits of using surveys is that you can rapidly and affordably contact many respondents. However, they have certain drawbacks, including the possibility of response bias and the difficulty in obtaining a representative sample.

Another effective technique for gathering data is experimentation, which is usually employed in scientific studies to demonstrate cause-and-effect linkages. In an experiment, researchers modify one or more independent variables and track the impact on a dependent variable after adjusting for confounding variables. Experiments can be conducted in field settings or controlled areas like labs. Experiments are most potent when they can reliably demonstrate causal linkages using random assignment and control. But, particularly in social and behavioral research, they can be resource-intensive and might only sometimes be practical or morally acceptable.

Without changing any of the factors, observational studies gather data by watching participants in their natural habitat. When conducting studies that would be impractical or unethical, this strategy would be beneficial. Studies using observational data can be unstructured, in which the researcher documents events as they happen, or structured, with predetermined standards for what is to be seen. Cross-sectional studies, which take a momentary picture of a population, and longitudinal studies, which follow the same individuals over time, are two examples of various observational studies. Although observational studies can yield rich, practical insights, their lack of control over factors makes them more prone to biases and impossible to demonstrate causality conclusively.

Web scraping is a contemporary method of gathering data that involves removing information from web pages. Due to the proliferation of the internet and the abundance of information it contains, this approach has become increasingly common. Although web scraping can be done manually, it is more frequently mechanized with software tools and programs that collect website data by methodically navigating them. This approach is constructive for rapidly and effectively gathering vast amounts of data. Frequently used applications include extracting information from social media, assembling news stories, and scraping product pricing from e-commerce sites. Web scraping must, however, be carried out morally and legally, as it may give rise to concerns about intellectual property and data privacy.

The network of linked devices that gathers and exchanges data is known as the Internet of Things (IoT). Examples of IoT devices are sensors, wearable technology, smart appliances, and industrial equipment. These devices continuously generate Real-time data streams, offering insightful information in various fields. IoT devices, for instance, may monitor home automation, security systems, and energy use in smart homes. Wearable technology in healthcare can monitor physical activity and vital signs, providing information on the health and behavior of patients. IoT sensors can monitor environmental factors and equipment performance in industrial environments, facilitating predictive maintenance and operational optimization. Strong data management and analytics capabilities are needed to extract valuable insights from the massive volume of data created by IoT devices.

Sensor data collection, which uses sensors to observe and record physical phenomena, is intimately associated with the Internet of Things. Numerous factors, including temperature, humidity, light, motion, and pressure, can be detected by sensors. Applications in healthcare, industry, and environmental monitoring all use this technique extensively. For example, industrial sensors monitor production lines and machinery, while environmental sensors monitor the weather and air quality. Sensors in the medical field can assess physiological characteristics, including glucose levels and heart rate. Sensor data is essential for real-time monitoring and decision-making due to its accuracy and dependability. However, managing and processing sensor data can be difficult because of the enormous volume and pace at which data is created take time and effort.

Every data collection technique has advantages and disadvantages, and the best approach will rely on the study's goals, the type of data that will be required, and pragmatic factors like time, money, and ethical issues. While surveys are a great way to get self-reported information on attitudes and behaviors, they can also have response bias. Although experiments can be resource-intensive and morally complex, they offer compelling evidence of causality. While observational studies provide valuable real-world insights, they must be sufficiently controlled to demonstrate definitive causality. Although it is an effective way to get a lot of online data, web scraping must be done legally and responsibly. IoT and sensor data collecting provide continuous, real-time insights, which requires strong data management and analytics infrastructure.

The incorporation of various techniques for gathering data can improve the accuracy and comprehensiveness of the information. For instance, merging observational and survey data can yield a more thorough picture of a research issue. Analogously, combining web-scraped data with sensor data can provide a more in-depth analysis of patterns and trends. The capacity to evaluate and comprehend data from various sources can be further improved using modern analytics and machine learning techniques.

To sum up, data gathering is an essential part of data science and analytics, and various approaches are accessible to fit varied circumstances and study goals. Conventional techniques, including experiments, surveys, and observational research, offer essential insights into people's attitudes, behaviors, and causal relationships. Contemporary methodologies, such as web scraping, IoT, and sensor data collecting, have novel prospects for acquiring substantial amounts of data in real-time from many sources. The quality and richness of data can be improved by comprehending the advantages and disadvantages of each approach and, where appropriate, integrating different ways, ultimately resulting in more innovative and well-informed decision-making. New techniques for gathering data will surface as technology develops, increasing the potential for data-driven insights and solutions.

Data Quality and Governance

Data quality and governance are essential elements of efficient data management. They guarantee that data is correct, comprehensive, and consistent. These components are necessary for enterprises to use their data assets to make trustworthy, well-informed decisions. Data governance frameworks and policies offer the structure and rules required to manage data quality, guarantee regulatory compliance, and promote enterprises' accountable and stewardship-focused culture.

The state of data in terms of its accuracy, consistency, and completeness is referred to as data quality. When data is accurate, it guarantees that the real-world objects or events it describes are accurately represented. Erroneous conclusions and poorly thought-out actions can result from inaccurate data, which can have grave ramifications for a company. The degree to which all necessary data is present is completeness. Incomplete analysis and false conclusions may arise from missing data. To avoid problems resulting from concurrent updates or data integration procedures, consistency entails ensuring that data is consistent and compatible across various datasets and systems.

High data quality demands ongoing validation and monitoring. Data profiling is one method for assessing several aspects of data quality, like correctness, consistency, and completeness. It entails examining data to find patterns, redundancies, and anomalies that might point to problems. Data profiling, for instance, can reveal outliers that point to mistakes or missing data that require attention. Organizations can uphold high data standards by conducting routine audits and quality assessments, which methodically identify and fix data problems.

Data governance administers an organization's availability, usability, integrity, and security. This process includes instituting guidelines, protocols, and benchmarks to guarantee that data is handled as a precious resource. Strong data governance ensures that data is dependable, safe, and easily accessible, which supports business goals and lays the groundwork for efficient data management.

A data governance framework usually consists of a few essential parts. It begins by outlining the obligations of the many parties engaged in data management. This covers users, custodians, owners, and stewards of data. While data owners can decide about certain data assets, stewards uphold governance standards and ensure high-quality data. The people who access and utilize the data for work are known as data users, while data custodians oversee the technical aspects of data storage and preservation.

Creating data policies and standards is crucial to a data governance framework. These policies describe the rules and regulations governing data management procedures, such as data entry, storage, access, and sharing. Data standards facilitate data integration and interoperability across many systems by ensuring uniformity in data formats, definitions, and classifications. For instance, a standard outlines the vocabulary used to categorize products or the format for date entries.

Putting data lifecycle management procedures into place is another aspect of data governance. This includes all aspects of the data journey, including production, acquisition, usage, storage, and disposal. Throughout its existence, data must be accurate, comprehensive, and relevant. This is ensured by effective data lifecycle management. Processes for validating, cleaning, enriching, archiving, and deleting data are all included. While data cleansing eliminates or fixes errors, data validation verifies information at the entry point for accuracy and completeness. By adding pertinent information, data enrichment improves data quality, and proper management of out-of-date or obsolete data is ensured by archiving and purging.

One of the most important aspects of data governance is ensuring data security and privacy. Organizations must shield sensitive information from misuse, unauthorized access, and breaches. This entails security measures like audit trails, access controls, and encryption. Regulations dictating how personal data should be gathered, processed, and stored, such as the California Consumer Privacy Act (CCPA) and the General Data Protection Regulation (GDPR), must be complied with by data privacy policies. In addition to defending people's right to privacy, compliance with these laws also shield corporations from fines and other consequences.

By guaranteeing that data remains secure and under control while being accessible to authorized users, data governance frameworks also aid in democratizing data. Data democratization makes data more accessible to a broader group of workers, enabling them to use it to inform decisions and promoting a data-driven culture inside the company. Organizations accomplish this by putting in place metadata management systems and data catalogs, which offer details about data assets, such as their location, quality, and usage policies. To ensure that users can use data accurately and effectively, metadata management helps users comprehend the context and meaning of the data.

A solid commitment to developing a data-driven culture and strong leadership are essential for effective data governance. Setting priorities for data governance efforts and obtaining the required funding and assistance depend on executive sponsorship. Councils or committees for data governance should be established by organizations, with representatives from a range of departments and roles. These councils manage data governance initiatives, address data-related concerns, and guarantee alignment with corporate goals.

Training and education are essential to promote data governance and quality practices. Workers should receive training on their roles and duties, the value of high-quality data, and data governance fundamentals. Workshops, seminars, and online courses can be incorporated into training programs to increase data competency and literacy throughout the company. Organizations can guarantee that all individuals comprehend the significance of data and their part in preserving its quality and integrity by cultivating a culture of accountability and stewardship.

Technology is a significant enabler for projects related to data governance and quality. Data governance tools and platforms make data categorization, lineage tracking, policy enforcement, and monitoring possible. Tools for data quality can be used to validate, clean, and profile data. Integrating data management and analytics technologies ensures that governance and quality processes are incorporated into the organization's data workflows. By automating data profiling, anomaly detection, and predictive data purification, cutting-edge technologies like artificial intelligence and machine learning can improve data quality.

Data quality and governance play a critical role in guaranteeing data accuracy, completeness, and consistency—a prerequisite for trustworthy decision-making. Frameworks and rules for data governance offer the organization and direction required for efficient data management, guaranteeing legal compliance and promoting a culture of responsibility and stewardship. Organizations may safeguard confidential information, advance data democratization, and uphold strict data standards through the lifecycle by implementing robust data governance procedures. Effective leadership, education, and utilizing cutting-edge technologies are essential for accomplishing quality and data governance projects. Effective data governance and quality management will be necessary to use data as a valuable asset and promote organizational success as it increases in volume and complexity.

CHAPTER III

Data Preparation and Preprocessing

Data Cleaning Techniques

Preprocessing and data preparation are essential phases in the data science pipeline that guarantee unprocessed data is converted into an organized and functional state for modeling and analysis. The data quality strongly influences the effectiveness and precision of machine learning models and analytical insights. For this reason, using efficient data cleaning methods, dealing with noise, outliers, and missing data, and normalizing and standardizing data are crucial to producing accurate results.

Data cleaning is known as finding and fixing mistakes, inconsistencies, and inaccuracies in the dataset. This step is crucial to enhance data quality and guarantee the ensuing analysis's validity. The existence of missing data is a prevalent problem in datasets. Missing data can result from several things, including intentional omissions, transmission problems, and mistakes made during data collection. Appropriate handling of missing data is essential since it might result in erroneous conclusions, lower statistical power, and skewed estimations. Missing data can be handled in several ways, such as deleting the data, imputation, and utilizing algorithms that naturally handle missing numbers.

Elimination entails deleting any rows or columns with missing values from the dataset. Although this approach is simple, a substantial amount of data may be lost, notably if a sizable fraction of the data needs to be included. As a result, it is usually only advised when there are very few missing data points. On the other hand, imputation entails substituting estimated values for missing ones in light of the existing data. Mean, or median imputation, is a widespread technique in which the corresponding feature's mean or median replaces missing values. More sophisticated methods include predicting and filling in missing values with machine learning models, which consider feature correlations and can produce more accurate estimates.

Data points that substantially differ from the rest of the dataset are called outliers. They may result from actual abnormalities, inaccuracies in the data collection process, or natural variability. Because outliers have the potential to skew statistical analyses and model performance, it is imperative to recognize and manage them. Several methods for identifying outliers include machine learning-based algorithms, statistical tests (such as Z-score and IQR), and visualization techniques like box and scatter plots. Outliers can be dealt with in several ways once they have been found. If they are thought to be incorrect, they can be eliminated, changed to lessen their impact, or handled differently if they are significant anomalies. The investigation's setting and particular objectives will determine which approach is best.

Errors or random fluctuations in data that mask the actual signal are called noise. Errors in measurement, data input, and the environment are only a few noise sources. Reducing noise is essential for improving the accuracy and durability of analytical models. Smoothing techniques (e.g., moving averages and Gaussian smoothing) help emphasize underlying patterns and smooth out random fluctuations. Furthermore, data transformation methods like the Box-Cox or log transformation can lessen the effect of noise and stabilize the variance.

Data normalization and standardization are two essential preprocessing methods that convert data to a standard scale without distorting variations in the ranges of values.

Known by another name, min-max scaling, normalization rescales the data to a predetermined range, typically [0, 1]. This technique ensures that no feature dominates the others in magnitude, especially when the features have diverse ranges and scales. To normalize a feature, subtract its minimum value and divide the result by the range (max-min). By ensuring that each component contributes equally to the study, this technique facilitates their comparison and combination.

Standardization, also known as Z-score normalization, transforms data to have a mean of zero and a standard deviation of one. This method works exceptionally well with techniques like k-means clustering and linear regression that presume typically distributed data. A feature's mean is subtracted, and the result is divided by the standard deviation to accomplish standardization. This technique can enhance the performance of numerous machine learning algorithms by ensuring that the data is distributed and scaled consistently.

Each approach has advantages and particular use cases. These are standardization and normalizing. The type of data and the needs of the study or model being utilized will determine which option is best. For example, normalization is frequently chosen when working with methods that are sensitive to the size of the data or when the data does not follow a normal distribution. Standardization is usually applied when the algorithm expects normally distributed features, or the data is typically distributed.

In addition to these methods, feature engineering—adding new features or changing preexisting ones to enhance model performance—is a common component of data preprocessing. Techniques like one-hot encoding for categorical variables, creating interaction terms, and deriving new features via domain-specific knowledge or mathematical transformations can all be a part of this process. Because feature engineering may significantly increase the prediction potential of machine learning models, it is an essential stage in the data preparation process.

Furthermore, dimensionality reduction methods like t-distributed Stochastic Neighbor Embedding (t-SNE) and Principal Component Analysis (PCA) are frequently used to decrease the number of features while maintaining the crucial structure of the data. These methods lessen computing complexity, lessen dimensionality's impact, and enhance models' interpretability. The maximum variance in the data is captured by a new set of orthogonal components that PCA creates from the original features. In contrast, t-SNE is especially helpful for visualizing high-dimensional data in lower-dimensional environments.

A thorough understanding of the data, the precise objectives of the analysis, and the properties of the selected algorithms is necessary for efficient data preparation and preprocessing. This dynamic, iterative process frequently entails switching between various stages to ensure the data is accurate, consistent, and ready for analysis. The ultimate objective is to convert unprocessed data into a format suitable for analysis and modeling, producing precise and trustworthy insights.

In summary, preprocessing and data preparation are crucial phases in the data science pipeline that guarantee unprocessed data is converted into an organized and useable format for modeling and analysis. Enhancing the quality and dependability of data requires using data-cleaning strategies, such as managing missing data, outliers, and noise. By putting data on a similar scale, normalization and standardization enable more precise and reliable analysis. The data's usefulness for predictive modeling is further improved via feature engineering and dimensionality reduction. Using these strategies, data scientists may guarantee that their analyses are grounded in high-quality data, producing more dependable and valuable findings. In the end, efficient preprocessing and data preparation help organizations make better decisions and accomplish strategic objectives by maximizing the use of their data assets.

Data Transformation

A crucial step in the data science process is data transformation, which includes improving the quality and relevance of raw data to get it ready for analysis. Data integration, data reduction, feature engineering, and feature selection are all included in this phase. These procedures are necessary to build efficient models and guarantee that the conclusions drawn from the data are precise and useful.

To enhance the functionality of machine learning models, feature engineering entails adding or changing new features. Since the objective of this method is to extract meaningful information from raw data that can improve predictive power, it mostly depends on subject expertise and imagination. Feature engineering, for instance, can entail collecting elements from a dataset containing timestamps, like the day of the week, month, or hour, to uncover temporal patterns pertinent to the research. Analogously, additional attributes in a dataset of consumer transactions can comprise the total amount spent, the typical purchase amount, or the frequency of purchases. These other characteristics add more context and strengthen the model's ability to identify underlying patterns in the data.

Another essential feature engineering component is converting categorical data into numerical form. Categorical data can be formatted for machine learning algorithms using methods like ordinal, one-hot, and label encoding. For instance, by generating binary columns for every category by one-hot encoding, algorithms can handle categorical data without presuming an innate order. This is especially crucial for algorithms that need numerical inputs, like support vector machines and linear regression.

The process of determining which attributes are most pertinent for model development is known as feature selection. It seeks to improve generalization and lessen overfitting in the model by eliminating unnecessary or duplicate characteristics. Several feature selection strategies are available, such as filter, wrapper, and embedding. Independent of any particular model, filter methods use statistical tests or correlation metrics to assess the significance of features. For example, techniques such as mutual information, Pearson correlation coefficients, and Chi-square tests can be used to find the attributes with the strongest correlations to the target variable.

Conversely, wrapper approaches entail training a model using various feature subsets and choosing the subset that produces the best results. Despite being computationally demanding, this iterative method can successfully determine the ideal feature set for a given model. Common wrapper approaches include forward or backward feature selection and recursive feature elimination (RFE). Feature selection is incorporated into the model training procedure through embedded approaches. By punishing complexity, regularization approaches such as Lasso (L1 regularization) and Ridge (L2 regularization) enhance model performance and choose features by default by decreasing the coefficients of less significant features to zero.

The process of merging data from several sources to produce a single, cohesive dataset is known as data integration. This phase is essential when data is gathered from several systems, departments, or even companies. Comprehensive analysis is made easier with effective data integration, guaranteeing that all pertinent information is available in a single, coherent dataset. In this process, disparities in granularity levels, units of measurement, and data formats are frequently reconciled. For example, harmonizing currency units and matching the data to a standard period may be necessary when merging sales data from various countries.

Data integration challenges include handling duplication, inconsistencies, and discrepancies between databases. Data cleaning techniques are crucial during this stage to resolve discrepancies and guarantee the accuracy and consistency of the integrated dataset. Advanced data integration tools and platforms offer three functions: schema matching, entity resolution, and data fusion. These functions automate many of these activities and improve the accuracy and speed of the integration process.

Data reduction strategies aim to minimize the number of characteristics or records in a dataset while preserving as much pertinent information as feasible. This is especially crucial for high-dimensional datasets since excess features might cause the dimensionality curse, which hurts model performance. A popular dimensionality reduction method called Principal Component Analysis (PCA) converts the original features into a new collection of orthogonal components known as principal components that capture the highest variation in the data. PCA successfully lowers the dataset's dimensionality while keeping most of the original data by keeping only the top few principal components.

Additional methods for reducing dimensionality are t-distributed Stochastic Neighbor Embedding (t-SNE) and Linear Discriminant Analysis (LDA). Finding the linear feature combination that best divides a given class is the goal of lattice distance analysis (LDA), which is mainly utilized in classification assignments. In contrast, t-SNE is a non-linear method that works well for two- or three-dimensional high-dimensional data visualization. Maintaining the data's local structure lowers dimensionality and facilitates the discovery of patterns and clusters.

Data reduction can entail lowering the number of records in addition to the number of features. For this, clustering, aggregation, and sampling are frequently employed. Choosing a representative subset of the data is known as sampling, and it can be beneficial when dealing with massive datasets. When data is consolidated, it is summarized at a finer level of detail. For example, daily sales data can be combined to provide monthly totals. By putting related entries in one group, clustering helps simplify the data and draw attention to key trends.

Building reliable and accurate models requires effective data transformation, which includes feature engineering, selection, integration, and reduction. It necessitates technical proficiency, topic knowledge, and thorough data comprehension. Data scientists can improve the predictive capability of their models by developing additional characteristics and picking the most pertinent ones. Data from many sources can be integrated to guarantee that all relevant information is available for analysis, and the dataset's dimensionality and complexity can be decreased to enhance interpretability and model performance.

Moreover, because data transformation is ongoing, we frequently must review and improve these procedures when new data becomes available or as our understanding of the issue changes. The efficacy and efficiency of the data transformation process can be significantly increased by utilizing sophisticated tools and techniques such as dimensionality reduction approaches, data integration platforms, and automated feature engineering and selection algorithms.

To sum up, data transformation is an essential stage in the data science process that includes a variety of methods for getting raw data ready for modeling and analysis. While data integration guarantees a complete and coherent dataset, feature engineering and selection improve the data's relevance and predictive value. Data reduction approaches enhance the interpretability and performance of models by addressing the issues of high dimensionality and massive datasets. These procedures guarantee that data is converted into a format that optimizes its potential to produce precise and valuable insights, promote innovation, and guide well-informed decision-making.

Tools and Technologies

Making well-informed judgments in today's data-driven environment requires the capacity to clean, preprocess, and analyze data effectively. Data scientists and analysts use various tools and technology to complete these jobs. The most well-liked and potent tools are SQL, R, and Python. These programs provide robust statistical analysis, data processing, and visualization capabilities. Furthermore, specialist software for preprocessing and data cleaning guarantees data quality and enables efficient data analysis.

Python is one of the most popular data science and analytics programming languages. Its widespread appeal results from its adaptability, simplicity of use, and vast ecosystem of frameworks and libraries explicitly designed for data analysis and manipulation. Several libraries, including Pandas, NumPy, and SciPy, offer robust functions for statistical analysis, data manipulation, and cleaning. In particular, Pandas is well-known for its capacity to manage enormous datasets and carry out intricate operations using an easy-to-understand vocabulary. Data scientists can easily manage missing values, combine datasets, execute group operations, and modify data frames when using Pandas. In addition, many machine learning projects employ Python's sci-kit-learn module, which provides a variety of methods for dimensionality reduction, regression, clustering, and classification. The production of visually appealing and educational graphs and charts is made possible by visualization frameworks like Matplotlib and Seaborn, which facilitate the discovery and sharing of data insights.

R is another vital tool frequently used in data science, which is especially useful for statistical analysis and data visualization. R is a tool for statisticians and data analysts because it offers a complete statistical computing and visualization environment. The language's syntax is ideal for carrying out intricate statistical analyses, and many packages, such as ggplot2, tidy, and dplyr, make data handling and visualization more accessible. For instance, the dplyr package offers several methods for data wrangling, making it simple for users to connect, filter, and summarize datasets. On the other hand, the ggplot2 program is well known for its capacity to produce intricate and adaptable visuals, allowing analysts to communicate data findings successfully. Furthermore, R's ability to be integrated with other technologies and tools, including Python and SQL, increases its adaptability and makes it a valuable tool for data scientists.

The standard language for maintaining and querying relational databases is called SQL, or Structured Query Language. It is essential for complicated searches and aggregations and data extraction, transformation, and loading (ETL) procedures. Data scientists can work directly with databases using SQL, retrieve pertinent data, and carry out several activities to prepare for analysis. When working with relational databases, SQL is a vital tool for data professionals due to its efficient handling of enormous volumes of data. Because of its relatively simple syntax, users may easily do tasks like filtering, sorting, grouping, and connecting tables. Additionally, how SQL integrates with other computer languages—like Python and R—makes data workflows more fluid and boosts the general effectiveness of data analysis jobs.

To ensure data quality and prepare data for analysis, specific software for data cleaning and preprocessing is essential in addition to these fundamental tools. One such tool is Open Refine, an open-source program for transforming and cleaning data. With Open Refine, users may inspect and purge jumbled data, find and fix discrepancies, and convert data into an organized format. It is a valuable tool for data preprocessing because of its extensive features and easy-to-use interface. These capabilities include performing transformations across big datasets and clustering techniques for spotting duplicate entries. Trifacta Wrangler is another well-liked application, a data-wrangling platform that uses machine learning to automate data transformation and cleaning chores. Users can rapidly profile, clean, and enhance data with Trifacta Wrangler's interactive and visual interface, which saves time and effort while preparing data.

Another powerful tool for data preparation is Alteryx, which offers a complete platform for data analytics, blending, and cleansing. Users can create workflows with Alteryx to automate processes related to data preparation, such as loading, transforming, and extracting data. The tool makes data preparation simple with its drag-and-drop interface and an extensive library of pre-built connectors and transformations, freeing users to concentrate on extracting insights from their data. Alteryx is a complete data science and analytics solution since it provides sophisticated analytics features like predictive modeling and geographic analysis.

Tools such as Informatica and Talend offer robust data integration and quality management features, making them ideal for enterprises looking for enterprise-grade preprocessing and cleaning solutions. With the help of Talend's range of solutions for data integration, data quality, and data governance, businesses can ensure that their data is accurate and consistent. With an easy-to-use interface, Talend's data preparation tool enables users to clean and transform data, and its data quality features assist in locating and fixing problems with the data, such as duplication, inconsistencies, and missing values. In contrast, Informatica offers a complete platform for managing data that includes master data management, data integration, and data quality tools. Organizations may profile, clean, and standardize data with Informatica's data quality solutions to ensure it satisfies the requirements for accuracy and completeness.

Cloud-based data preparation solutions have become more popular in recent years due to their scalability and accessibility. Programs like Google DataPrep and AWS Glue offer cloud-native solutions for data cleaning and preprocessing, which let users take advantage of the cloud's capacity to handle big datasets and intricate transformations. While AWS Glue offers a fully managed ETL service that automates data preparation processes and connects smoothly with other AWS services, Google DataPrep, developed with Trifacta, offers a simple interface for exploring, cleaning, and transforming data.

The discipline has also seen a revolution by incorporating machine learning (ML) and artificial intelligence (AI) into data cleaning and preprocessing techniques. AI-powered solutions can drastically reduce the amount of human labor needed for data preparation by automatically identifying and fixing problems with the data, such as outliers, missing numbers, and inconsistencies. Through machine learning algorithms, these tools can learn from data and gradually enhance their performance, leading to more accurate and efficient data cleaning and preprocessing.

In summary, many tools and technologies that simplify data cleaning, preprocessing, and analysis have improved data science and analytics. The fundamental tools for data processing, statistical analysis, and database administration are Python, R, and SQL, each of which has advantages. Preprocessing and data cleaning specialized software, such as Alteryx, Trifacta Wrangler, and Open Refine, offers reliable solutions for guaranteeing data quality and getting data ready for analysis. Enterprise-grade tools like Talend and Informatica provide comprehensive data management capabilities, while cloud-based and AI-powered solutions improve scalability and efficiency. Combined, these tools and technologies enable data professionals to turn unstructured data into insightful knowledge that promotes innovation in the digital era and helps decision-making.

CHAPTER IV

Exploratory Data Analysis (EDA)

Introduction to EDA

An essential phase in the data science process is called exploratory data analysis (EDA), which entails looking through and visualizing data to find underlying patterns, anomalies, correlations, and insights. EDA, which statistician John Tukey first presented in the 1970s, has become a fundamental component of data analysis and is a basis for additional statistical and machine-learning modeling. Understanding the data structure, spotting outliers, testing underlying hypotheses, and gaining a sense of intuition about the dataset are the main goals of exploratory data analysis (EDA). This comprehension aids in the clarification of theories and directs the choice of suitable modeling methodologies.

EDA starts with a description of the dataset, covering its dimensions, different kinds of variables, and preliminary views of its distribution. This initial phase typically entails importing the dataset into an appropriate environment and doing preliminary inspections, such as R's or Python's Pandas data frame. Essential summary statistics provide a numerical dataset summary, including mean, median, standard deviation, and range. Furthermore, graphical representations provided by visual tools like scatter plots, box plots, and histograms can shed light on potential data distribution problems, like skewness or outliers.

It is impossible to exaggerate the value of EDA. Analysts can find flaws and inconsistencies, such as missing numbers, duplication, or inaccurate data entries, by carefully going over the data. These issues must be fixed before moving on with additional research. Understanding the correlations between variables is easier using EDA, which is useful when creating predictive models. Pairwise scatter plots and correlation matrices, for example, can show linear or non-linear connections between features, which can help in feature engineering and selection. EDA also helps identify trends and patterns that aren't always evident, including seasonality in time-series data or clusters in multi-dimensional data, which can reveal necessary information about the underlying processes producing the data.

To completely comprehend the data, several repeated and systematic rounds of analysis are frequently necessary during the EDA process. Data cleaning is the initial phase, which includes treating outliers, fixing errors, and finding and handling missing numbers. Missing values can be handled in several ways, from simple imputation using mean or median values to more complex approaches like multiple imputations or algorithms specifically designed to handle missing data. Statistical techniques like Z-scores and the IQR method, as well as visual aids like box plots, are used to detect outliers, which have the potential to skew results and model performance. Depending on their nature and significance, outliers can be eliminated, changed, or handled differently after they have been detected.

Univariate analysis, which looks at each variable separately, comes after data cleansing. Calculating summary statistics and producing visuals are part of this study to comprehend each variable's distribution and central tendency. For continuous variables, histograms, box plots, and density plots are frequently utilized; for categorical variables, bar charts and pie charts are typically employed. Understanding the distribution of the data, spotting odd trends, and determining whether the data satisfies the presumptions needed for additional statistical analysis are all aided by univariate analysis.

After univariate analysis, bivariate and multivariate analysis examines the connections between two or more variables. Examining the relationship between two variables is known as bivariate analysis, and it frequently makes use of cross-tabulations or bar charts for categorical data and scatter plots for continuous variables. Correlation coefficients, such as Pearson or Spearman correlation, measure the direction and intensity of linear correlations between continuous variables. Chi-square tests and contingency tables are valuable tools for analyzing connections between categorical variables. This is extended to more than two variables through multivariate analysis, which visualizes interactions and dependencies among several variables using methods including heatmaps, pairwise scatter plot matrices, and three-dimensional displays. Principal Component Analysis (PCA) and cluster analysis are examples of advanced statistical approaches that can be used to comprehend the relationships and structure found in high-dimensional data.

The visualization of the data is a crucial component of EDA. Visualizations offer an intuitive grasp of data linkages and patterns, which may be evident and obscure from numerical summaries alone. It is easier to communicate findings and hypotheses when visual aids such as histograms, box plots, scatter plots, and heatmaps effectively highlight patterns, anomalies, and outliers. Deeper insights into the data can be facilitated using tools such as ggplot2 in R or Matplotlib, Seaborn, and Plotly in Python. These tools offer a wide range of static and interactive visualization creation capabilities.

Testing underlying data assumptions is another aspect of EDA. Many statistical techniques and models assume the data has specific correlations or distributions. For example, homoscedasticity usually distributes errors, and a linear relationship between the dependent and independent variables is considered in linear regression.

EDA uses tests and diagnostic charts to evaluate these assumptions. For instance, residual plots can detect deviations from linearity and check for homoscedasticity, while Q-Q plots can assess normalcy.

Documenting observations and findings is not just a personal task, but an essential part of the collaborative EDA process. Noting any problems with the quality of the data, summary statistics, infographics, and preliminary theories or insights are all included in this documentation. Maintaining thorough documentation ensures that every action is transparent and repeatable, fostering cooperation and enabling a more methodical approach to data analysis. Additionally, this material is a great resource for enhancing analysis and guiding upcoming modeling projects, contributing to the collective knowledge of the data science community.

To sum up, exploratory data analysis is an essential step in the data science process that allows for continuous learning and improvement. It enables you to fully comprehend the data, uncover underlying correlations and patterns, and spot problems that need fixing before moving on to more in-depth research. Data cleansing, univariate, bivariate, and multivariate analysis, visualization, and assumption testing are just a few of the methodical processes that EDA offers as a strong basis for creating dependable insights and strong statistical models. Because EDA is iterative, you can continually improve your comprehension of the data, which will help you make better decisions and produce significant outcomes. EDA will become more and more crucial in revealing significant insights and promoting data-driven decision-making as data volume and complexity continue to rise.

Descriptive Statistics

A dataset's properties can be summarized and understood in large part through the use of descriptive statistics. Descriptive statistics give a thorough picture of the data and help analysts spot patterns, trends, and possible anomalies using measures of central tendency and variability and data distribution analysis. Making educated decisions and laying the groundwork for more intricate inferential statistics and data analysis methods depend on these statistical tools.

The center point of a dataset is described by measures of central tendency, which offer a single number that symbolizes the usual or average observation within the data. The three main metrics used to assess central tendency are the mean, median, and mode. By adding up each value in a dataset and dividing the total by the number of observations, one can determine the mean, also known as the arithmetic average. It is commonly utilized because of its simplicity and capacity to condense data into a single figure. The mean, however, is susceptible to outliers, which can distort the result and obscure the data's underlying tendency. For instance, given a dataset of incomes where the majority of people make between $40,000 and $60,000, a small number of people with much higher incomes may inflate the mean, creating the appearance of a higher total income.

Conversely, the middle value in a dataset arranged from lowest to highest is known as the median. The median is the central value in an odd number of observations in the dataset; it is the average of the two central values in an even number of observations. The median provides a more accurate measure of the central tendency for skewed distributions since it is resistant to outliers. For example, in the previously described income dataset, the median would represent the middle of the income distribution, untouched by very high numbers, giving a more accurate image of the average income level.

The value that appears the most frequently in a dataset is its mode. Although the mode can help identify the most prevalent value in categorical data, it provides less information in continuous data, mainly when there are no repeating values or numerous modes (bimodal or multimodal distributions). However, the mode might provide helpful information in certain situations, such as determining the most popular category in a survey or the most often bought item in a sales record.

The spread or distribution of data points about the central tendency is described by measures of variability, also known as dispersion. The primary metrics used to quantify variability are the variance, standard deviation, interquartile range (IQR), and range. The difference between a dataset's maximum and minimum values is known as the range, the most fundamental indicator of variability. Although the range gives a rapid impression of the spread of the data, it is not sensitive to the distribution of values within the dataset. It is, therefore, quite susceptible to outliers.

The gap between the first quartile (25th percentile) and the third quartile (75th percentile) is the interquartile range (IQR), which quantifies the dispersion of the middle 50% of the data. Because it is unaffected by extreme values, the IQR is more reliable than the range. It gives a better view of the variability around the median by briefly summarizing the data's central dispersion.

Standard deviation and variance are more complete measures of variability. The average squared deviation of each data point from the mean is quantified by variance, which gives an idea of the degree of variation among the values in the dataset. More excellent higher variance indicates greater dispersion, whereas a lower variance suggests closeness to the mean. This dispersion is expressed in the same units as the original data by the standard deviation, the square root of variance, which facilitates interpretation. When applied to normally distributed data, the standard deviation can shed light on the likelihood of witnessing particular values within given ranges. For instance, in a normal distribution, around 95% of data points fall between two standard deviations and 68% fall within one standard deviation of the mean.

Analyzing data distribution entails looking at the distribution and form of the data to identify any underlying trends. The histogram is a popular tool for visualizing data distribution since it shows the frequency of data points within designated intervals or bins. The shape of the distribution—whether symmetric, skewed, unimodal, bimodal, or multimodal—can be seen using histograms. Like a normal distribution, the data points in a symmetric distribution are dispersed equally around the mean. On the other hand, a skewed distribution has a large tail on one side, which suggests that the data points are focused on that side.

Box-and-whisker charts, often known as box plots, are an additional helpful technique for displaying data distribution. They show the median, quartiles, and possible outliers while summarizing the central tendency and variability of the data. The box represents the IQR, the line inside the box shows the median, and the whiskers reach the lowest and most excellent values within 1.5 times the IQR. Plotting individual data points outside this range is done as they are regarded as outliers. Box plots work very well for comparing distributions across several groups or categories.

Density plots help determine the form and distribution of continuous data because they offer a smoothed estimate of the data distribution. They give a more accurate depiction of the distribution's underlying structure and are independent of bin width and placement, unlike histograms. They can also draw attention to characteristics that histograms might not be able to, like multimodality or skewness.

Descriptive statistics and data distribution analysis are more significant than simple summaries. They are the cornerstone for inferential statistics, model construction, and hypothesis testing. Comprehending the central tendency and variability facilitates the selection of appropriate statistical tests and models, the evaluation of data assumptions, and guarantees the validity of inferences made from the data. For example, statistical procedures, including ANOVA and t-tests, assume homoscedasticity (equal variance) in normally distributed data. These presumptions are supported by descriptive statistics, which also aid in test selection and interpretation.

Descriptive statistics and distribution analysis are also essential for evaluating data quality. Finding trends, anomalies, and inconsistencies might draw attention to data quality problems, requiring additional research and repair. For instance, a dataset with exceptionally high variability may contain measurement errors or data entry problems that should be fixed before further analysis.

Descriptive statistics—which comprise measures of central tendency and variability—and data distribution analysis are crucial to summarizing and comprehending data. They give analysts a thorough picture of the dataset's features, allowing them to spot trends, patterns, and anomalies. By using these tools, analysts may guarantee the validity and dependability of their conclusions, make well-informed decisions, and direct the selection of suitable statistical tests and models. Data workers will always need to be able to use descriptive statistics to adequately summarize and evaluate data because data is becoming more and more relevant in many different industries when it comes to making decisions.

Visualization Techniques

Data analysis requires visualization tools because they offer a way to see patterns, trends, and insights that may take time to be clear from raw data alone. Data are visually represented by graphs and charts, which facilitate the understanding and accessibility of complex information. Good data visualization helps reveal essential patterns and improves the dissemination of research results to a larger audience. These visualizations can be made with various tools, each with advantages and strengths. Tableau, a flexible data visualization tool, and the Python utilities Matplotlib and Seaborn are the most well-known.

In exploratory data analysis (EDA) and other contexts, graphs and charts are essential for turning abstract data into visual narratives. They assist analysts in finding connections, patterns, outliers, and clusters within datasets. Scatter plots, for example, help analyze the relationship between two continuous data since they can show possible outliers, clusters, and correlations. When displaying time-series data, line graphs are frequently used to show patterns and trends across time. These can be used to identify long-term trends, seasonality, and cyclic behaviors. However, for distribution and categorical analysis, respectively, bar charts and histograms work well. While histograms display the distribution of a continuous variable, demonstrating the frequency of data points within given ranges, bar charts compare amounts across distinct categories.

Matplotlib is one of the core and most used libraries in the Python ecosystem and one of the tools for making these visuals. Matplotlib, created by John D. Hunter, offers a complete set of tools for creating interactive, animated, and static visualizations. Many data scientists and analysts choose it because of its convenience and versatility. Every plot element, from the most basic ones like lines and markers to the more complex ones like axes, labels, and comments, maybe finely customized with Matplotlib. This degree of control is beneficial when producing figures that must follow precise formatting requirements and are of publishing quality. The visualization process is also streamlined by Matplotlib's interface with other Python libraries like NumPy and Pandas, which provide smooth data handling and modification.

Another Python tool called Seaborn enhances the versatility and customization of Matplotlib by providing a more advanced interface for creating visually appealing and educational statistical visuals. Seaborn, developed by Michael Waskom, is primarily for statistical data visualization. It offers pre-installed color schemes and themes to enhance the visual appeal of Matplotlib's default plots. Complex visualizations like violin plots, heatmaps, and pair plots—especially helpful for deciphering correlations in multivariate data—can be made more easily with Seaborn. For example, heatmaps are used to show matrix-like data, where the color intensity of the data represents the variable's magnitude. Violin plots provide information about the distribution and probability density of the data by combining the advantages of box plots and kernel density charts. Pair plots, also known as scatterplot matrices, make it possible to see pairwise correlations between several variables in one image, which makes an extensive exploratory investigation easier.

Outside of the Python community, Tableau is a solid and approachable data visualization tool for technical and non-technical users. Without needing to know a lot of programming, users can create dynamic and interactive visualizations with Tableau thanks to its drag-and-drop interface. Because of its accessibility, Tableau has become well-known in business intelligence and analytics, where it is essential to communicate data insights quickly and effectively. Extensive dataset handling, multiple data source integration, and the creation of interactive dashboards that let users delve down into data, filter views, and gain deeper insights are Tableau's key differentiators. Tableau dashboards are especially helpful for presentations and reports because of their interactivity, which allows stakeholders to examine the data and extract relevant insights for their purposes.

Effective visualization creation takes more than selecting the appropriate tool; it also necessitates comprehending the data and the narrative being told. Compelling visualizations follow the guidelines of precision, efficiency, and clarity. Instead of needless intricacy that could mislead the audience, they should be made to accurately and concisely convey the main points. For instance, applying strategies like color-coding or faceting—separating the data into several sub-plots according to a categorical variable—can help make sense of a disorganized scatter plot with excessive data points.

It is also very important to select the appropriate kind of visualization. Bar charts and pie charts are more suitable for comparing values across different categories, but scatter plots and line graphs are great for illustrating relationships and trends. Bubble charts and heatmaps can represent additional dimensions, adding more context and depth to the data. The type of visualization selected should align with the kind of data and the particular insights intended to be highlighted.

In reality, the process of producing visualizations typically begins with data cleaning and preparation, which is then followed by exploratory analysis that uses straightforward plots to determine the relationships and structure of the data. Now, tools like Matplotlib and Seaborn are beneficial because they enable rapid iterations and modifications. Tableau can generate more polished and interactive visuals after the exploratory phase, mainly if the objective is to deliver findings to stakeholders or a larger audience who might benefit from interactive data exploration.

In conclusion, data visualization techniques are critical for revealing patterns and insights within the data, turning uninterpreted numerical data into visually compelling narratives. Robust tools for producing a variety of static and statistical graphics, such as Python's Matplotlib and Seaborn, offer flexibility and aesthetic improvements for in-depth exploratory study. Tableau is an excellent tool for creating dynamic representations that improve data exploration and communication in business situations because of its intuitive interface and robust interactive capabilities. The selection of appropriate technologies is one factor that affects how effective data visualization is; other factors include the careful use of design principles that guarantee relevance, accuracy, and clarity. Finding insights and coming to wise conclusions depend heavily on the capacity to visualize data efficiently, even as data science develops.

CHAPTER V

Statistical Foundations for Data Science

Probability Theory

The cornerstone of data science is statistical foundations, which offer fundamental ideas and instruments for data analysis, inference, and decision-making in the face of uncertainty. Probability theory, a mathematical framework for measuring uncertainty and comprehending the likelihood of different events, is fundamental to these foundations. Most statistical analysis is based on probability theory, which helps data scientists forecast, evaluate risks, and simulate real-world phenomena.

Comprehending random events, their outcomes, and the likelihood that they will occur are essential to understanding probability fundamentals. The symbol P represents an event's probability ranging from 0 (an impossible occurrence) to 1 (a specific event). The notation P(A) represents the probability of an event A. For instance, P(Heads) = 0.5 is the probability of landing heads when tossing a fair coin, which is valid for tails. This straightforward idea applies to more complicated situations where it is necessary to consider the sample space—collecting all potential outcomes. There are six possible outcomes in the sample space when rolling a die. The probability of rolling a specific number, like 4, is P(4) = 1/6.

There are three ways to approach probability: classical, frequentist, and Bayesian. The classical method uses equal likelihood and symmetry to determine probability, making it appropriate for clearly specified issues with known outcomes. Probability is defined by the frequentist method as the long-term relative frequency of an event occurring in multiple trials. For example, drawing cards several times and tracking the frequency of red cards can be used to empirically assess the likelihood of receiving a red card from a well-shuffled deck of cards. In contrast, the Bayesian approach views probability as a measure of confidence or certainty about an event that is updated in light of new information. A key component of Bayesian probability, the Bayes theorem offers a way to update prior beliefs in light of observed facts, which makes it especially helpful in dynamic and unpredictable situations.

The difference between independent and dependent events is a basic idea in probability theory. Events classified as independent are those whose occurrence or non-occurrence has no bearing on one another. For instance, successive flips of a fair coin are independent occurrences; the result of one toss has no bearing on the outcome of the subsequent ones. On the other hand, dependent events are impacted by one another. For example, whether or not an ace was drawn as the first card in a deck of cards affects the likelihood of drawing an additional ace.

The way probabilities are given to various outcomes in the sample space is described by probability distributions. Depending on whether there are countable or uncountable possible outcomes, these distributions can be either discrete or continuous. Discrete probability distributions, like the Poisson and binomial distributions, apply to situations where the potential consequences are discrete and limited. The number of successes in a fixed number of independent Bernoulli trials, such as the number of heads in several coin flips, is modeled by the binomial distribution, defined by the parameters n (number of trials) and p (probability of success in each trial). The Poisson distribution describes the likelihood of a specific number of events occurring in a predetermined period or place, such as the number of phone calls a call center receives in an hour, which has an average rate of occurrence (λ) parameter.

The normal, exponential, and uniform probability distributions are examples of continuous probability distributions applicable to situations where the results can have any value within a range. In statistics, the normal distribution—also referred to as the Gaussian distribution—may be the most significant. It is distinguished by a bell-shaped curve, where the standard deviation (σ) determines the spread, and the mean (μ) serves as the curve's center. Because of the central limit theorem, which asserts that the sum of a large number of independent, identically distributed random variables tends to follow a normal distribution regardless of the original distribution of the variables, the normal distribution is used to model many natural phenomena and serves as the basis for many statistical techniques.

When events happen continuously, independently, and at a constant average rate in Poisson, the exponential distribution with parameter λ represents the interval between occurrences. Reliability analysis and queuing theory frequently use it to simulate object lifetimes or waiting times. Random numbers are generated in simulations using the uniform distribution, a basic model for random occurrences where all outcomes in a range have an equal chance of occurring.

In data science, probability distributions are valuable tools beyond simple theoretical understanding. They are employed in hypothesis testing, model uncertainty, and concluding populations from sampling. Data scientists, for instance, use the binomial distribution in A/B testing to examine experiment results and assess the efficacy of various product or feature variations—the Poisson distribution aids in quality control by keeping track of the number of manufacturing process flaws.

Furthermore, point estimates and confidence intervals can be used to estimate population parameters using probability distributions. Because of these characteristics, the normal distribution is widely employed in hypothesis testing and confidence interval construction. For example, the Z-test and t-test, based on the normal distribution, are used to compare means and determine the significance of observed differences in sample data.

With a firm reliance on probability distributions, Bayesian statistics offers a versatile framework for revising beliefs and making uncertain choices. Bayesian approaches have become increasingly popular in data science because they can account for past knowledge and adjust to new data—applications for methods like Bayesian networks and inference range from machine learning and predictive modeling to medical diagnostics.

Distributions and probability theory are fundamental to machine learning. Probabilistic models, like Naive Bayes classifiers, use probability distributions to forecast the likelihood of various outcomes depending on input information. Utilizing probability distributions, hidden Markov models (HMMs) and Gaussian mixture models (GMMs) represent sequences and clusters, respectively, opening up applications in anomaly detection, speech recognition, and natural language processing.

To sum up, probability distributions and theory are crucial parts of the statistical framework underpinning data science. They offer the ideas and instruments required to model actual occurrences, measure uncertainty, and arrive at wise conclusions. Data scientists can examine data, make conclusions, and create predictive models by applying ideas ranging from discrete and continuous distributions to fundamental probability. Probability theory's incorporation into statistical techniques and machine learning highlights its importance for solving challenging issues and advancing data-driven fields. A thorough grasp of probability and its applications will be essential for deriving significant insights and making wise decisions in an unpredictable world as data science develops.

Inferential Statistics

A subfield of statistics known as inferential statistics enables us to extrapolate conclusions and forecasts about a population from a sample of data. Statisticians can test hypotheses, evaluate the uncertainty of these estimates, and draw conclusions regarding population parameters by employing inferential procedures. Confidence intervals and hypothesis testing are the two main instruments used in inferential statistics. These ideas are fundamental to evaluating the dependability of decisions made using data and making data-driven decisions themselves.

A formal process called hypothesis testing compares observable facts with a hypothesis, the integrity we wish to determine. The null hypothesis (H0), which stands for a claim that there is no effect or difference, is the hypothesis that has to be tested. The null hypothesis, for instance, can claim that the medication does not affect patients' health if we wish to determine whether a new medication is helpful. We seek to conclude the alternative hypothesis (H1 or Ha) if the null hypothesis is sufficiently refuted. Keeping the medication example going, the alternate theory is that the medication does affect patients' health.

The first step in the hypothesis testing procedure is to choose a significance level (α), usually set at 0.05. This level indicates the likelihood of rejecting the null hypothesis if it is true (Type I mistake). The next step is to gather data and calculate a test statistic, which expresses the degree to which the observed data differ from the expected data under the null hypothesis. Depending on the test, this statistic may or may not follow a particular probability distribution, such as the t-distribution or the normal distribution.

A crucial idea in hypothesis testing is the p-value. It shows the likelihood that, under the null hypothesis, test results will be at least as dramatic as the observed outcomes. A low p-value provides evidence against H0 by indicating that the observed data are unlikely under the null hypothesis. If the p-value is smaller than the selected significance threshold (α), the alternative hypothesis is accepted, and the null hypothesis is rejected. For example, we reject the null hypothesis that there is no difference in efficacy between the approaches. We find a statistically significant difference if a study comparing two teaching methods provides a p-value of 0.03 and α is set at 0.05.

Confidence intervals serve as a valuable tool in conjunction with hypothesis testing by offering a range of values within which the proper population parameter lies. Unlike hypothesis testing, which provides a binary choice (reject or fail to reject H0), confidence intervals provide an estimate with a set confidence level. For example, a 95% confidence interval suggests that approximately

95% of the confidence intervals we generate from many samples contain the proper population parameter.

The sample statistic (such as the sample mean), the statistic's standard error, and the crucial value from the relevant probability distribution (such as the z-value from the normal distribution or the t-value from the t-distribution) must all be determined before building a confidence interval. The sample statistic is then multiplied by the critical value and the standard error to get the confidence interval. For instance, we would add and subtract the margin of error—the crucial value times the standard error—from the sample mean to create a 95% confidence interval. With a 95% confidence level, this interval offers a range likely to contain the population mean.

There is a strong correlation between hypothesis testing and confidence intervals. If the 95% confidence interval for a mean difference does not include zero, a statistically significant difference at the 0.05 significance level is shown. On the other hand, if the interval contains zero, there is insufficient data to rule out the null hypothesis that there is no difference. Because of this relationship, confidence intervals and hypothesis tests can be interpreted consistently, guaranteeing the validity and dependability of the results.

Comprehending the underlying assumptions of inferential statistics is imperative for their appropriate utilization. Confidence intervals and hypothesis tests usually depend on specific data assumptions, like independence, homoscedasticity (equal variance), and normality. If these presumptions are fixed, accurate results may result. For example, the t-test, particularly with small sample sizes, presupposes that the data are regularly distributed. The test findings may only be valid if this assumption is met. Alternative techniques that don't rely on certain distributional assumptions, like non-parametric testing, may be appropriate in these situations.

In addition, p-value interpretation needs to be done carefully. A p-value does not measure the probability that the observed facts happened by accident or that the null hypothesis is true. It just shows how well the data supports the null hypothesis. Consequently, a low p-value does not confirm the alternative hypothesis but indicates evidence against the null hypothesis. Furthermore, it has been said that the arbitrary significance level of 0.05 fosters a dichotomous interpretation of research findings that could be abused and misinterpreted.

Moreover, multiple hypothesis testing calls into question the reliability of p-values. There is a greater chance of making at least one Type I error when conducting several tests. To mitigate this danger of false positives, techniques like the Bonferroni correction modify the significance threshold to take the number of tests into consideration. The trade-offs in statistical testing are highlighted because these modifications may also make Type II mistakes (failing to reject a false null hypothesis) more likely.

In conclusion, inferential statistics offer solid tools for making inferences about populations from sample data, including confidence intervals and hypothesis testing. P-values estimate the strength of the evidence against a null hypothesis in hypothesis testing, providing an organized framework for doing so. Confidence intervals estimate the range that the proper population parameter falls into by adding a degree of uncertainty to hypothesis testing. Combined, these techniques help researchers and data scientists measure uncertainty, make well-informed decisions, and guarantee the validity of their conclusions. Proper implementation and interpretation of these methods necessitate a deep comprehension of their presumptions, constraints, and the background of the data under examination. The fundamentals of inferential statistics are still essential to thorough and trustworthy data analysis, supporting evidence-based decision-making across a broad range of domains as statistical approaches continue to develop.

Regression Analysis

The foundation of statistical modeling is regression analysis, which includes logistic and linear regression methods that are essential for deciphering correlations between variables and generating predictions from observed data. A popular technique for simulating the relationship between a dependent variable and one or more independent variables is linear regression. It assumes that the predictors and the response variable have a linear relationship to determine the best-fitting line across the data points. Slope coefficients (β) and an intercept term ($\beta0$) that describe this line are estimated from the data using techniques like ordinary least squares (OLS). A variety of scenarios can benefit from the versatility and applicability of linear regression, including the analysis of the effect of advertising expenditure on sales revenue and the prediction of house prices based on features such as size and location.

For the model estimates to be legitimate, however, several presumptions underlying linear regression must be satisfied. These presumptions include residual normalcy, homoscedasticity, linearity, and independence. According to the assumption of linearity, there is a linear relationship between the independent and dependent variables, which means that changes in one predictor variable cause corresponding changes in the response variable. Inaccurate forecasts and skewed parameter estimates may result from breaking this premise. The independence assumption states that the error components are uncorrelated and that the residuals, or the variations between the observed and predicted values, are independent. This assumption is broken by autocorrelation, which occurs when the residuals correlate and might produce skewed and wasteful estimates.

The assumption of homoscedasticity, also known as the constant variance of residuals, is that the residual distribution is continuous at all levels of the independent variables. This assumption is broken by heteroscedasticity, which occurs when the variance of the residuals varies across levels of the independent variables. This can result in skewed parameter estimates and inaccurate standard errors. The assumption of residual normality states that the residuals have a constant variance and a zero mean, according to a normal distribution. Deviations from normalcy can impact the accuracy of confidence intervals and model-based hypothesis tests. Even though linear regression can withstand modest deviations from normalcy, large deviations can produce skewed parameter estimates and untrustworthy conclusions.

On the other hand, when the dependent variable is categorical, or binary as opposed to continuous, logistic regression is utilized. Based on one or more predictor factors, a binary outcome's probability is modeled using logistic regression. It is frequently used to simulate outcomes like the presence or absence of disease, customer turnover, or loan default in industries including epidemiology, marketing, and finance. By restricting the predicted probabilities to the interval [0, 1], the logistic function is used in logistic regression to estimate the likelihood of the binary outcome. The exponentiated values of the model coefficients, or odds ratios, give comprehensible measurements of how the predictors affect the odds of the event. The model coefficients represent the log odds of the outcome occurring.

Like linear regression, logistic regression depends on presumptions to guarantee the model's validity. These presumptions include the logit's linearity, the observations' independence, the lack of multicollinearity, and the absence of significant outliers. The logit's linearity presupposes a linear relationship between the independent factors and the dependent variable's log odds. This assumption can be evaluated by looking at plots of the logit (log odds) against the independent variables. Assuming that every observation is independent of the others or that the occurrence of one observation does not affect the occurrence of another is known as the independence of observations theory. The validity of standard errors and hypothesis testing in logistic regression depends heavily on this premise.

High correlations between independent variables are referred to as multicollinearity, and they can inflate the standard errors of the regression coefficients and cause instability in the estimations. Measures like correlation matrices and the variance inflation factor (VIF) can be used to identify multicollinearity. The assumption that no single observation significantly affects the estimated coefficients and predictions is the lack of influential outliers. It is crucial to locate outliers and deal with them effectively, either by eliminating them or applying robust regression procedures, as they can alter the estimated coefficients and impair the model's fit.

Evaluating regression models' assumptions is crucial to guaranteeing the accuracy and dependability of the findings. Diagnostic tools are available to evaluate these assumptions and find possible model problems. To evaluate linearity, independence, and homoscedasticity in linear regression, residual analysis entails plotting the residuals against the independent variables or the predicted values. The model's overall fit can be evaluated using goodness-of-fit tests, such as the Breusch-Pagan test for heteroscedasticity or the Durbin-Watson test for autocorrelation. Similar diagnostic techniques can be used for logistic regression, including residual analysis, multicollinearity tests, and influential outlier checks.

To sum up, regression analysis includes logistic and linear regression methods, which are essential for predicting outcomes based on observed data and modeling relationships between variables. Both methods depend on assumptions to guarantee the models' validity, and diagnostics are critical for evaluating these presumptions and spotting possible problems with the model. By comprehending and taking care of these assumptions and diagnostics, researchers and analysts can guarantee the dependability and robustness of their regression analyses, derive significant conclusions, and make well-informed decisions from the data.

CHAPTER VI

Machine Learning Basics

Overview of Machine Learning

A subset of artificial intelligence called machine learning has revolutionized several industries by fostering innovations and efficiency that were previously unthinkable. The fundamental component of machine learning is the creation of algorithms that allow computers to learn from and make predictions or judgments based on data. This section will give an overview of machine learning, along with information on its definition, the three primary learning styles (supervised, unsupervised, and reinforcement learning), and essential terms and concepts necessary to comprehend this area of study.

One definition of machine learning is a data analysis technique that automates the creation of analytical models. It is a subfield of artificial intelligence that is predicated on the notion that machines can learn from data, spot patterns, and make judgments with little help from humans. Large volumes of data are sent into a computer algorithm throughout the learning process, and the system uses the analysis and insights to produce predictions or judgments. By "learning" from experience, the algorithm becomes more adept at making correct predictions as it processes more data.

Generally speaking, there are three forms of machine learning: reinforcement, unsupervised, and supervised. Each species is suited for various jobs because of its distinct qualities and uses.

The most prevalent kind of machine learning is supervised learning. A labeled dataset is used to train the model, meaning that each training example has an output label. By reducing the discrepancy between its predicted and actual output, the model can map inputs to the desired output. Iteratively, this process is carried out until the model reaches high accuracy. Regression and classification are the two primary subtasks of supervised learning. Predicting a discrete label, such as whether or not an email is spam, is the process of classification. Conversely, regression entails making predictions about a continuous variable, like determining a house's price depending on its attributes. Some supervised learning algorithms include neural networks, support vector machines, logistic regression, and linear regression.

On the other hand, unsupervised learning works with unlabeled data. The goal is to identify incoming data's inherent structures or hidden patterns. Without labels to direct the learning process, the algorithm tries to figure out the fundamental structure of the data on its own. In unsupervised learning, dimensionality reduction and grouping are frequent problems. Image compression and market segmentation benefit from grouping comparable data points together produced by clustering techniques like K-means and hierarchical clustering. High-dimensional data can be more easily visualized by using dimensionality reduction techniques such as Principal Component Analysis (PCA) and t-distributed Stochastic Neighbor Embedding (t-SNE), which decrease the number of random variables under consideration. Unsupervised learning is essential in domains where data classification could be more apparent.

In reinforcement learning, an agent gains decision-making skills by acting in a way that maximizes a concept of cumulative reward in its environment. Reinforcement learning learns from the results of its actions rather than labeled input/output pairs like supervised learning does. Through interaction with the surroundings and feedback in the form of rewards or penalties, the agent modifies its behavior to maximize future benefits. This kind of learning is beneficial in scenarios like gaming, robotics, and autonomous driving, where the order of activities matters. The policy establishes the agent's behavior; the reward signal, which gives feedback on the effectiveness of action; and the value function, which calculates the predicted future rewards, are essential ideas in reinforcement learning. In reinforcement learning applications, algorithms like Proximal Policy Optimization (PPO), Deep Q-Networks (DQN), and Q-learning are frequently utilized.

Gaining a deeper understanding of machine learning requires familiarity with key terms and ideas. One basic idea is the training set, or dataset, used to train a machine learning model. To guarantee that the model performs effectively when applied to fresh, untested data, this dataset must represent the issue space. Model performance is closely linked to the ideas of overfitting and underfitting. When a model learns the training set too thoroughly—including noisy and outlier data—it is said to be overfitting, leading to poor generalization of fresh data. Underfitting occurs when a model performs poorly on both the training and test datasets because it is too simplistic to identify the underlying patterns in the data.

Another crucial idea is the test set, a different subset of the dataset that the model does not encounter during training. It is employed to assess the model's effectiveness and guarantee that it adapts adequately to fresh data. Cross-validation is a technique that divides the data into various subsets and uses some of those subsets for training and some for validation to analyze the model's performance more robustly. This procedure aids in reducing the variance found in the performance review.

Hyperparameters, such as the learning rate, the number of hidden layers in a neural network, or the number of clusters in K-means clustering, are configurations that need to be established before the learning process starts. These are not the same parameters the algorithm picks up during training. Hyperparameter tuning determines which hyperparameters work best for a model and can significantly impact the model's performance.

Regularization involves adjusting the loss function to include a penalty for more significant model coefficients to stop overfitting. Methods like Lasso (L1 regularization) and Ridge (L2 regularization) are frequently employed for this. A crucial idea in machine learning is feature engineering, which selects, modifies or creates new features from the raw data to enhance the machine learning model's performance. Practical feature engineering can have a significant impact on the model's efficacy.

To sum up, machine learning is an effective tool for data analysis and decision-making with applications in many fields. Each of its three primary forms—supervised, unsupervised, and reinforcement learning—offers special techniques for resolving various issues. Creating efficient machine learning models requires a thorough understanding of key terms and ideas like regularization, hyperparameters, overfitting and underfitting, training and test sets, and feature engineering. Keeping up with these fundamentals will be essential to realizing the full potential of machine learning as the field develops.

Supervised Learning Algorithms

A core component of machine learning is supervised learning, a practical process of training models using labeled data to make predictions or categorize data points. Classification and regression, the two main categories of tasks in supervised learning, are practical tools for data analysis. To address these problems, supervised learning frequently employs a number of practical techniques, such as support vector machines (SVM), decision trees, and k-nearest neighbors (KNN). This section will offer a thorough analysis of these practical methods, emphasizing their uses, benefits, and functions, to empower you in your data analysis journey.

Among the most popular and easily understood algorithms in supervised learning are decision trees, a versatile tool that can adapt to various data types. A decision tree is a structure that resembles a flowchart, with each internal node denoting a feature test, each branch representing the test's result, and each leaf node representing a continuous value or class label. Classification rules are reflected in the routes that lead from the root to the leaves. Decision trees are very useful due to their ease of use and readability. They don't need feature scaling and can handle both category and numerical data. Decision trees divide data into subsets according to the input feature values in a classification context, with the goal of maximizing information gain at each split. When performing regression tasks, the tree averages the values of the samples in a particular leaf to forecast the continuous value.

Decision trees, despite their simplicity, are not without challenges. Especially when the tree is allowed to grow deeply without being pruned, they have a tendency to overfit the training set. By deleting branches that have low predictive potential for the target variable, pruning techniques like cost complexity pruning can reduce overfitting. Furthermore, because even slight changes in the input might result in completely different trees, decision trees can be unstable. These challenges can be overcome by ensemble techniques such as gradient boosting and random forests, which combine the predictions of several decision trees to increase robustness and accuracy. Being aware of these challenges makes you better prepared for your data analysis tasks.

Another well-liked supervised learning technique for regression and classification is K-nearest neighbors (KNN). Since KNN is an instance-based and non-parametric learning method, it does not explicitly learn a model. It does not make any significant assumptions about the distribution of the underlying data. Instead, the KNN predicts the new data point by comparing it to its closest neighbors in the training dataset. The technique classifies a new data point by allocating the most prevalent class among its k-nearest neighbors. Regression predicts the continuous output by averaging the values of the k-nearest neighbors.

KNN's main benefits are its ease of use and efficiency, particularly with smaller datasets. It is simple to use and naturally capable of handling multi-class categorization issues. KNN, however, has several things that could be improved. The distance measure, the number of neighbors taken into account, and the choice of k all substantially impact the system's performance. Manhattan, Minkowski, and Euclidean distances are examples of standard distance measures. Moreover, because KNN needs to calculate the distance between each new data point and every training point, it can be computationally costly, particularly as the training dataset gets more extensive. Data architectures like ball trees and KD trees, which increase the effectiveness of nearest-neighbor searches, can help lessen this.

Although they can also be modified for regression, support vector machines (SVM) are robust supervised learning algorithms mainly employed for classification tasks (also known as support vector regression or SVR). SVM aims to locate the ideal hyperplane in the feature space that maximizes the margin between various classes. The margin can be defined as the separation between the nearest support vectors (data points) from each class and the hyperplane. SVM improves the model's generalization capacity by ensuring the decision boundary is as far away from any data point as feasible.

SVM works extremely well in high-dimensional domains and is resistant to overfitting, especially when there are more dimensions than samples. The algorithm can perform both linear and non-linear classification. SVM employs kernel functions, such as the sigmoid, polynomial, and radial basis function (RBF), to transform the data into a higher-dimensional space where a linear hyperplane can divide the classes to perform non-linear classification. The kernel trick is a method SVM uses to construct intricate decision boundaries.

Even with its advantages, SVM has its challenges. It requires solving a quadratic optimization problem, which can be computationally demanding, particularly for gigantic datasets. The regularization parameter (C) and kernel parameters are examples of hyperparameters that affect the model's performance and must be carefully chosen. This is usually done by cross-validation. Furthermore, SVM lacks probabilistic estimations of class membership, which may be a disadvantage in some situations.

In conclusion, classification and regression are the two main task types in supervised learning, which include a range of algorithms built to forecast outcomes based on labeled data. Although they provide a clear and understandable method, decision trees are unstable and prone to overfitting. K-nearest neighbors can be computationally intensive and parameter-sensitive, but they offer simplicity and effectiveness, especially for smaller datasets. Through the kernel technique, support vector machines provide stable performance, particularly in high-dimensional areas, but they come with a high processing cost and need careful parameter tweaking. Selecting the best approach for a particular problem requires understanding these algorithms' advantages and disadvantages. This will ultimately help in the creation of precise and successful predictive models in the field of supervised learning.

Unsupervised Learning Algorithms

An important area of machine learning is unsupervised learning, which is the modeling and analysis of data without predetermined labels. This kind of learning aims to find hidden structures or patterns in the data. In unsupervised learning, association and grouping are the two main tasks. While association focuses on finding intriguing associations between variables in massive datasets, clustering entails organizing data points into clusters based on commonalities. K-means, hierarchical clustering, and the Apriori algorithm are a few of the most well-known and often applied algorithms among the many others created for these kinds of problems. This paper investigates various algorithms, examining their workings, benefits, drawbacks, and uses.

Partitioning a dataset into groups, or clusters, so that data points within the same cluster are more similar to each other than those in different clusters is the goal of clustering, an essential task in unsupervised learning. K-means is one of the most widely used clustering techniques. The dataset is to be divided into k unique, non-overlapping clusters using the K-means clustering algorithm. The procedure begins by randomly initializing k centroids—the clusters' centers. After that, each data point is matched with the closest centroid to create k clusters. The mean of every data point in each cluster is used to recalculate the centroids. Iteratively allocating points and recalculating centroids is done until the centroids stop changing noticeably, indicating that the clusters are stable.

Large datasets can benefit from K-means' ease of implementation and computational efficiency. It is not without restrictions, though. Understanding the data beforehand makes it easier to specify the number of clusters, k. Additionally, K-means is sensitive to the centroids' initial placement, which might produce varying clustering outcomes for various initializations. It also assumes that clusters are uniformly sized and spherical, which may only be valid for some datasets. Notwithstanding these drawbacks, k-means is a popular tool for several tasks, such as anomaly detection, market segmentation, and picture reduction.

Another crucial method for clustering is hierarchical clustering. Hierarchical clustering does not require the number of clusters to be predetermined, unlike k-means. Instead, it creates a hierarchy of clusters that may be visualized as a dendrogram, a figure that resembles a tree and preserves the orders of merges and splits. Agglomerative and divisive hierarchical clustering are the two primary varieties. Each data point begins in its cluster in a bottom-up technique called agglomerative clustering. Iteratively, pairs of clusters are combined based on how similar they are to one another until only one cluster is left. Conversely, divisional clustering is a top-down method in which every data point begins in a single cluster and is then divided into smaller clusters by a recursive process.

Because agglomerative clustering is so simple to implement, it is employed more frequently. Several linkage criteria, including single linkage (minimum distance), complete linkage (maximum distance), and average linkage (average distance), can be used to quantify the similarity between clusters. By slicing the dendrogram at the appropriate level, hierarchical clustering generates a dendrogram that visually shows the data structure, facilitating the process of determining how many clusters to include. However, compared to k-means, hierarchical clustering requires more computing power, making it less appropriate for big datasets. Additionally, noise and outliers might cause it to become sensitive, which can skew the final clusters. Notwithstanding these difficulties, hierarchical clustering is functional for grouping related genes and analyzing gene expression data in bioinformatics and other domains.

An alternative kind of unsupervised learning called association rule learning concentrates on finding intriguing connections, or associations, between variables in sizable datasets. A popular and well-established technique for mining association rules is the Apriori algorithm. It works on the tenet that every subset of a frequent itemset must likewise be frequent. Finding frequently occurring itemsets and producing association rules from these itemsets are the two primary processes of the method. In the first phase, the algorithm searches the dataset iteratively to identify itemsets that satisfy a minimal support threshold or the percentage of transactions that contain the itemset. It then generates rules in the second stage based on a conditional likelihood of a transaction containing some things also containing other items, known as the minimal confidence threshold.

The Apriori algorithm is highly efficacious in market basket analysis when used to find products that regularly co-occur in consumer interactions. Recommendation engines, cross-selling, and product placement are just a few uses for this information. The Apriori algorithm has its restrictions, though. It can be computationally costly because it necessitates numerous data scans, particularly for massive datasets. Additionally, the algorithm produces many candidate item sets, many of which might not be noteworthy or helpful. The Apriori method is nevertheless an essential resource in the field of association rule learning despite these shortcomings.

To sum up, unsupervised learning is the application of several algorithms to find latent patterns and structures in data that do not have labels assigned to them. The two fundamental tasks in this field are clustering and association; the most widely used techniques are k-means, hierarchical clustering, and the Apriori algorithm. K-means clustering is simple and effective, although it might be sensitive to initialization and needs to know how many clusters there are beforehand. Although it has a higher computational complexity and is more noise-resistant, hierarchical clustering visually represents the data structure. It does not require the number of clusters to be defined in advance. The Apriori approach can be computationally demanding and produce many candidate item sets, but it helps find connections between variables, especially in market basket analysis. It is essential to comprehend these algorithms' workings, benefits, and constraints to apply unsupervised learning methods to a wide range of real-world issues.

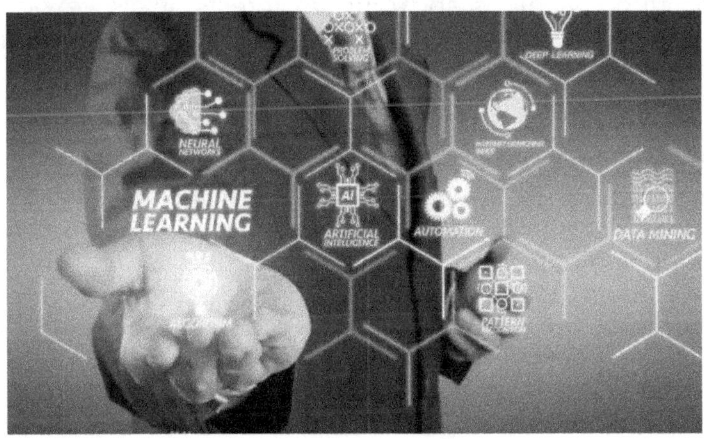

CHAPTER VII

Advanced Machine Learning Techniques

Ensemble Methods

With its rapid evolution, machine learning has introduced a plethora of methods for data analysis and predictive modeling. Among these, ensemble methods have garnered significant interest due to their ability to enhance the performance and robustness of individual models. By combining several models, ensemble approaches provide more dependable and accurate predictions. This paper delves into various techniques, with a focus on practical applications such as gradient-boosting machines and random forests. It also explores their advantages, disadvantages, and real-world applications, underscoring their relevance in the field of predictive modeling and data analysis.

An ensemble technique called bagging, or bootstrap aggregating, is intended to lower variance and stop machine learning models from overfitting. The basic idea underlying bagging is to use bootstrapping, which involves sampling with replacement to build several subsets of the original training data. The next step is to train a different model using each subgroup, usually of the same type. All models' predictions are combined to get the final prediction, often done by majority vote for classification tasks or average for regression assignments. Because each model only sees a different fraction of the data, bagging can reduce variance by producing a variety of models that, when combined, can make more stable and broadly applicable predictions.

One of the most often used bagging techniques, random forests, applies the concept of bagging to decision trees. Many decision trees are trained on bootstrapped subsets of the data in a random forest. By choosing a random subset of attributes to account for each split in the trees, random forests also provide extra randomization to the mix. This correlation between the trees improves the model's performance as a whole. Random forests work incredibly well when dealing with massive datasets with high-dimensional feature spaces. They offer insights into feature relevance, strong resistance to overfitting, and exceptional accuracy. They can, however, be memory- and computationally intensive, mainly when there are a lot of trees. Applications for random forests are numerous and include bioinformatics, financial modeling, and image and speech recognition.

Another effective ensemble technique, "boosting," combines weak learners to produce a strong learner to lower bias and variation. In contrast to bagging, which trains models independently, boosting trains models sequentially, with each new model aiming to fix the mistakes of the previous one. An initial model is trained using the complete dataset at the beginning of the process. The same data is used to train subsequent models, but they focus more on cases that the earlier models misclassified. This iterative procedure is carried out until a certain number of models are trained or the model's performance stops improving. All models' projections are combined to create the final forecast, frequently by average or weighted voting.

Gradient boosting machines, or GBMs, are a widely used boosting implementation. GBMs develop models stepwise, training each new model to forecast the residual errors of the ensemble of earlier models. This is accomplished using gradient descent or other optimization of a loss function. One of GBMs' advantages is their adaptability to various loss function types, which enables them to be used for multiple applications such as regression, classification, and ranking. High predicted accuracy and adaptability to complicated datasets with heterogeneous variables are hallmarks of GBMs. They may, however, be vulnerable to overfitting, especially if there are a lot of iterations. To reduce overfitting, regularization strategies like shrinkage (learning rate) and tree trimming are frequently used. GBMs are widely utilized in many fields, including marketing for consumer segmentation and recommendation systems and finance for credit scoring and risk assessment.

Stacking, also known as stacked generalization, is a sophisticated ensemble technique that integrates several models by using the outputs of base models to train a meta-model for prediction purposes. When stacking, base models' predictions are utilized as input features for the meta-model after they have been trained on the original dataset. After that, the meta-model—typically a straightforward logistic or linear regression—is trained to forecast the result. The theory behind this is that to increase overall performance, the meta-model may figure out how to best integrate the basic models' predictions. Stacking is a highly adaptable approach that can incorporate machine learning approaches with various base models, such as boosting and bagging algorithms.

There are various benefits to stacking. Combining the advantages of several models can identify a more extensive variety of relationships and patterns in the data. Additionally, it enables the fusion of many model types, including decision trees, support vector machines, and neural networks, which can be very helpful in cases when the underlying data distribution is complicated. Stacking must be carefully adjusted to prevent overfitting and can be computationally costly. For stacking to be successful, base models and the meta-model must be adequately trained and validated. This approach is frequently utilized in machine learning competitions, such as those organized by Kaggle, where attaining the maximum accuracy possible is crucial.

To sum up, ensemble approaches are now considered essential in machine learning since they provide reliable and precise results for various predictive modeling applications. Combining many models trained on bootstrapped datasets, known as bagging—best represented by random forests—lowers variance and improves model stability. Gradient boosting machines are examples of how boosting successively trains models to fix mistakes, resulting in excellent predicted accuracy and efficient handling of complicated datasets. By integrating various base models via a meta-model, stacking increases the power of ensemble methods and captures a wider variety of patterns and correlations in the data. All these methods have unique benefits and drawbacks, making them appropriate for various issues and uses. Comprehending and utilizing these sophisticated machine learning methodologies is essential to constructing cutting-edge predictive models capable of handling the intricacies of real-world data.

Neural Networks and Deep Learning

Artificial intelligence has revolutionized thanks to neural networks and deep learning, which have made significant strides possible in several areas, like image identification, natural language processing, and autonomous systems. Neural networks are computational models built to identify patterns and learn from data modeled after the human brain's structure. Neural networks with multiple layers, or deep neural networks, are machine learning capable of capturing complex patterns and representations in massive datasets. An overview of neural networks is given in this section, which focuses on the designs, uses, and functions of two popular varieties:

recurrent neural networks (RNNs) and convolutional neural networks (CNNs).

Layers of connected nodes, or neurons, make up neural networks, which process incoming data and provide an output. To add non-linearity to the model, each neuron takes in input from several other neurons, applies a bias and a weighted sum, and then passes the outcome through an activation function. Neural networks can simulate intricate correlations in the data thanks to this technique. An input layer, one or more hidden layers, and an output layer are commonly seen in the architecture of a neural network. Neural networks use algorithms such as backpropagation—which minimizes the gap between the expected output and the actual target values by iteratively updating the parameters to reduce error—to change the weights and biases during training.

A specific kind of neural network called a convolutional neural network (CNN) handles data that resembles a grid, such as photographs. CNNs' effectiveness in tasks requiring visual data can be attributed to their capacity to learn spatial hierarchies of features automatically and adaptively. The convolution operation, which includes applying several filters to the input data to build feature maps, is the fundamental concept underlying CNNs. By swiping over the input data, these filters—kernels— perform element-wise multiplications and sum the outcomes to identify local patterns like edges, textures, and forms.

Convolutional, pooling and fully linked layers are among the various layer types that commonly make up a CNN's architecture. Using the convolution process, convolutional layers remove features from the input data. By reducing the spatial dimensions of the feature maps, pooling layers —often via procedures like max pooling or average pooling—reduce the number of parameters and computational costs while maintaining crucial information. Lastly, fully linked layers allow the network to learn high-level representations and generate predictions by tying every neuron in one layer to every other layer's neuron.

Computer vision has advanced dramatically as a result of CNNs. They have attained cutting-edge performance in tasks including object detection, picture segmentation, and image classification. CNN, for instance, forms the foundation of famous designs like AlexNet, VGGNet, and ResNet, which have established industry standards in image recognition contests. In addition to image analysis, CNNs are used for tasks including video analysis, natural language processing, and medical image processing, all of which need data representation in a grid-like format.

In contrast, sequential data—where the order of data points matters—is the domain of recurrent neural networks (RNNs). RNNs differ from ordinary neural networks in that they feature directed cycle connections, allowing them to retain a memory of past inputs. For problems involving time series data, language modeling, and sequence prediction, RNNs are especially well-suited. The primary characteristic of RNNs is their capacity to share parameters throughout many time steps, which enables them to handle variable-length sequences.

An RNN's architecture consists of input, hidden, and output layers. The hidden layer is connected to both the input at that moment and the secret state that came before it. Thanks to this recurrent connection, the network can keep a concealed state that records details about the prior time steps. By using a backpropagation through time (BPTT) technique, which modifies the weights to minimize the prediction error over all time steps, the backpropagation algorithm is expanded to handle sequences during training.

Standard RNNs have limitations when capturing long-term dependencies because of things like vanishing and expanding gradients. More sophisticated RNN variations, such as gated recurrent units (GRUs) and long short-term memory (LSTM) networks, have been created to overcome these issues. By introducing memory cells and gating techniques to regulate input flow, LSTMs effectively mitigate the vanishing gradient problem and allow the network to retain crucial information across longer sequences. GRUs combine the forget and input gates into a single update gate to reduce the number of parameters while maintaining performance, simplifying the LSTM design.

Numerous sequential data problems have seen the successful application of RNNs and their derivatives. They are employed in text production, machine translation, and language modeling in natural language processing. For example, applications such as Google's Neural Machine Translation system and OpenAI's GPT series have been made possible by RNN-based models. RNNs have increased the accuracy of text transcription from spoken words in voice recognition. RNNs are also used in time series forecasting to forecast other temporal phenomena, such as weather patterns and stock prices.

CNNs and RNNs are two examples of how deep learning can use sequential and hierarchical processing to turn unstructured data into insightful knowledge. These networks' success is primarily due to their capacity to automatically learn representations from data, eliminating the need for labor-intensive manual feature engineering. However, massive, labeled datasets and significant computer resources are needed for deep neural network training, which can be a drawback in particular applications. Some of these obstacles have been lessened by developments in hardware, such as graphics processing units (GPUs) and specialized AI accelerators, as well as methods like data augmentation and transfer learning. This has allowed for more acceptance and innovation.

In summary, convolutional and recurrent neural networks have led to breakthroughs in image and sequence processing, and deep learning and neural networks have significantly influenced artificial intelligence. While RNNs and their variants successfully capture temporal correlations in sequential data, they are also crucial in advancing natural language processing and time series analysis. CNNs are highly skilled at extracting spatial characteristics from grid-like data, which makes them invaluable in computer vision tasks. By pushing the limits of what machines can learn and do, these architectures' continual development and improvement hold the potential to open up new possibilities and applications.

Model Evaluation and Optimization

The machine learning workflow's essential model optimization and evaluation elements guarantee that the created models are precise and broadly applicable. While optimization strategies improve the model's predictive power, practical evaluation sheds light on the model's performance. This paper explores the significance of model evaluation, the different types of cross-validation used, and the procedures related to model selection and hyperparameter tweaking.

The process of evaluating a machine learning model's performance on a dataset is known as model evaluation. To fit the model, the available data is divided into training and testing sets, with the testing set being used to assess the model's performance. The most critical metrics for assessment differ according to the task. Still, they usually include mean squared error, mean absolute error, or R-squared for regression tasks, and accuracy, precision, recall, and F1 score for classification tasks. Although these metrics offer a preliminary assessment of the model's performance, they do not ensure that it performs well when applied to new data.

Cross-validation is a more reliable method of evaluating models, which reduces the possibility of overfitting and yields a more accurate estimate of the model's generalization performance. K-fold cross-validation is the most popular cross-validation technique. To do k-fold cross-validation, split the dataset into k folds or subsets. On k-1 folds, the model is trained, and on the remaining fold, it is validated. Every fold serves as the validation set once during the k iterations of this operation. To estimate the model's performance with greater accuracy, the performance metrics are averaged over all k iterations. Common variants include leave-one-out cross-validation (LOOCV), where k is set to the number of data points, meaning that each validation set consists of a single point, and stratified k-fold cross-validation, which guarantees that each fold has a similar distribution of classes and is especially helpful for imbalanced datasets.

Determining a model's ideal collection of hyperparameters is known as hyperparameter tuning. Unlike model parameters learned during training, hyperparameters are the parameters established before the learning process starts. The regularization parameter, the number of neurons and hidden layers in a neural network, and the learning rate are a few examples of hyperparameters. These hyperparameters significantly affect the model's performance and generalizability; hence, it is critical to tune them correctly. Several techniques are used for hyperparameter tuning, such as grid search, random search, and Bayesian optimization.

An exhaustive search method called "grid search" entails creating a grid of hyperparameter values and assessing the model's performance for each set of values. This approach guarantees that every potential combination is examined; nonetheless, it may incur significant computing costs, mainly when dealing with numerous hyperparameters or a broad range of values. In contrast, random search is more efficient than grid search and frequently produces equivalent results since it samples a certain number of hyperparameter combinations from the defined grid. A more advanced method called Bayesian optimization balances exploration with exploitation to more effectively locate the optimal set. It creates a probabilistic model of the hyperparameter space and uses it to identify the most promising hyperparameters to evaluate next.

Model selection evaluates a group of candidate models to determine which model performs best using validation data. This approach is essential because different models may have differing degrees of complexity and presumptions about the data. While non-linear models such as decision trees or neural networks better capture complicated patterns, linear models, for instance, may be easier to understand. In addition to considering aspects like interpretability, computational economy, and resilience against overfitting, model selection criteria may also consider performance measures derived from cross-validation.

Model selection and optimization can also involve ensemble approaches, which aggregate predictions from various models. Methods such as bagging, boosting, and stacking combine the advantages of different models to enhance prediction performance. By training many models on multiple subsets of the data and averaging their predictions, bagging decreases variance. By progressively training models to fix their predecessors' mistakes, they are boosting aims to reduce bias. To identify more intricate patterns in the data, stacking entails training a meta-model to aggregate the predictions of basic models.

A crucial element in evaluating and optimizing models is tackling overfitting and underfitting. When a model learns the noise and specifics of the training data to the cost of its performance on fresh data, this is known as overfitting.

Underfitting occurs when a model is too essential to identify the underlying patterns in the data. By giving a more accurate estimate of the model's performance on hypothetical data, methods like cross-validation aid in detecting overfitting. To prevent overfitting, regularization techniques like L1 and L2 regularization include a penalty term to the loss function that limits the complexity of the model. To avoid co-adaptation and encourage robust learning, dropout, a regularization approach used in neural networks, randomly removes units during training.

Moreover, according to the machine learning equivalent of the "no free lunch" theorem, no single model is optimal for every situation. This highlights the significance of evaluating and choosing the suitable model, as various models have varying advantages and disadvantages based on the type of data and the task at hand. Decision trees, for example, are interpretable and perform well with categorical data but are susceptible to overfitting. On the other hand, support vector machines can efficiently handle high-dimensional spaces, although they might need to have their hyperparameters carefully adjusted.

Finally, time limits and computational resources are fundamental to model evaluation and optimization. Resource-intensive models and exhaustive search methods, such as grid search, may call for effective resource management and, occasionally, approximation techniques. To expedite these procedures, parallel processing and distributed computing are frequently used. Furthermore, by streamlining model evaluation, hyperparameter tuning, and selection through tools like AutoML, the machine learning process may be automated, making these sophisticated methods more approachable for individuals with varying degrees of machine learning experience.

In conclusion, creating reliable and accurate machine learning models requires careful consideration of model optimization and evaluation. Reliable estimates of model performance are provided by cross-validation techniques, including k-fold cross-validation, which also prevents overfitting. Methods for tuning hyperparameters, such as grid search, random search, and Bayesian optimization, are essential in determining which collection of hyperparameters is optimal for a particular model. In selecting a model, various factors, such as computational efficiency and interpretability, are considered, along with performance measures, to determine which model performs best. Developing well-generalizing models requires addressing overfitting and underfitting using methods such as regularization. A comprehensive and systematic approach to model evaluation and optimization guarantees the development of efficient and dependable machine-learning solutions, especially considering the variety of tasks and data.

CHAPTER VIII

Big Data Technologies and Ecosystem

Introduction to Big Data

Big Data has become a key component of today's digital environment, impacting business, scientific, and industrial decision-making and propelling technological advancements. Comprehending Big Data entails knowing its distinguishing features, sometimes summarized by the four Vs: volume, velocity, variety, and veracity. These features draw attention to the size and complexity of big data and the difficulties in handling and analyzing it. This paper examines big data fundamentals, examining what makes it unique and the significant challenges in handling large amounts of data.

The phrase "Big Data" describes datasets that are challenging to handle and process with conventional data processing tools and techniques due to their size, complexity, and rate of increase. Big Data includes a variety of data types and the speed at which data must be generated and processed in addition to enormous data volumes. The four Vs offer a thorough foundation for comprehending the complex nature of big data.

The most apparent feature of big data is volume. It illustrates the massive volume of data produced and kept. The amount of data generated daily is astounding due to the widespread use of digital devices, social media, sensors, and other data-generating sources. For example, every day, social media sites like Facebook and Twitter produce terabytes of data, while sectors like retail, healthcare, and banking generate enormous volumes of transaction and consumer data. The storage, retrieval, and analysis of such massive amounts of data are complex. The inadequacy of conventional databases and data processing tools in managing petabytes and exabytes of data frequently calls for creating distributed computing frameworks and scalable storage solutions.

The rate at which data is created, gathered, and processed is called velocity. Data is generated at previously unheard-of speeds in today's networked world, necessitating processing in real-time or very real-time. Financial transactions, website clickstreams, sensor data from Internet of Things devices, and social media feeds are a few examples. Systems that can ingest, process, and analyze data in real-time are required due to the high velocity of data in order to assist decision-making processes and offer timely insights. These demands have led to the development of technologies like Apache Kafka and real-time analytics platforms, which allow businesses to process streaming data and respond quickly to changing circumstances.

The variety includes all the various kinds and sources of data that make up big data. Big Data is a collection of structured, semi-structured, and unstructured data, unlike traditional datasets, which are frequently structured and easily fit into relational databases. Data in tables and spreadsheets is an example of structured data; it is well-organized and straightforward to search. Formats with some organizational characteristics but less rigidity than structured data, such as JSON and XML, are considered semi-structured data. Big Data mainly consists of unstructured data, which includes text, photos, videos, social media posts, and sensor data. This diversity makes integrating, storing, and analyzing data extremely difficult. Complex methods are needed to glean valuable insights from disparate data sources.

Veracity deals with the reliability and caliber of the information. Big Data frequently involves collecting data from multiple sources, which can lead to discrepancies, errors, and uncertainties. The accuracy of the data is vital since complete data might result in accurate assessments and better decision-making. Data cleaning, validation, and verification procedures ensure data authenticity to eliminate noise, fix mistakes, and reconcile inconsistencies. This is especially difficult in significant data contexts, where manual data quality checks are impracticable due to data generation's high volumes and rapidity. To ensure consistent data quality and trustworthy insights from Big Data, sophisticated algorithms, and automated technologies are necessary.

Beyond the four Vs, processing big data presents several other obstacles. One of the main obstacles is data administration and storage. Big Data's magnitude and complexity make traditional databases and storage solutions inadequate for the task. Distributed storage systems, like cloud-based storage options and Hadoop's HDFS, have made scalable and fault-tolerant storage possible. These systems disperse data among several nodes, guaranteeing data integrity and accessibility even in the case of hardware malfunctions.

There are also several obstacles in the way of data processing and analysis. The sheer amount and diversity of Big Data require sophisticated processing methods and substantial computer power. Due to their frequent shortcomings, traditional data processing methods gave rise to distributed computing frameworks such as Apache Hadoop and Apache Spark. Thanks to these frameworks, massive datasets may be processed in parallel across computer clusters, which significantly reduces data processing times and makes massive dataset analysis possible.

Processing large amounts of data is challenging because of the need to ensure data security and privacy. Protecting sensitive and personal data from breaches and unauthorized access is critical, given the growing volume of data being collected. Strict access controls, encryption, and data anonymization are crucial safeguards for personal information. Moreover, managing Big Data becomes even more challenging when adhering to data protection laws like the GDPR.

Integration of data is also another major obstacle. Large-scale data frequently originates from diverse sources, each possessing a unique format, schema, and semantics. Complex data integration methods and technologies are needed to combine this disparate data into a cohesive and unified picture. Data transformation, mapping, and reconciliation processes are involved to guarantee compatibility and consistency among various data sources.

Moreover, a persistent difficulty in big data systems is their scalability. Systems must scale well to handle growing loads as data quantities and processing requirements rise. In addition to scalable processing and storage options, this calls for a resilient infrastructure that can manage low latency and high throughput demands. Cloud computing now greatly facilitates scalability, which provides elastic and scalable resources as needed.

One more issue facing the Big Data ecosystem is the skills gap. Big Data technologies are sophisticated and specialized, requiring knowledge of data science, machine learning, distributed computing, and data engineering, among other fields. Nevertheless, firms find it difficult to fully utilize the potential of Big Data due to a lack of qualified personnel in these fields. Funding for education and training is essential to close this gap, as is encouraging business and academic cooperation.

In conclusion, significant data volume, pace, variety, and authenticity make it a transformational force in the digital age. These features draw attention to the size and complexity of big data, which in turn draws attention to the severe difficulties of processing, scalability, integration, privacy, and data storage. To tackle these obstacles, cutting-edge technologies, creative fixes, and qualified experts are needed. The Big Data ecosystem has the potential to significantly alter how we see and engage with the world as it develops by fostering innovation, insights, and well-informed decision-making in a variety of industries.

Hadoop Ecosystem

The Hadoop ecosystem, which provides a scalable and robust framework for organizing and analyzing big datasets, has emerged as a critical component of Big Data processing. The Apache Software Foundation created Hadoop, which offers various components and tools to manage the enormous amounts of data produced in the modern digital era. The Hadoop Distributed File System (HDFS), MapReduce, and Yet Another Resource Negotiator (YARN) are the three main parts of the Hadoop system. Every component is essential to enable the effective resource management, processing, and storage required for Big Data applications.

The core of the Hadoop ecosystem is the Hadoop Distributed File System (HDFS), which was created to store massive datasets in a distributed setting. Data is partitioned into blocks by HDFS and dispersed among several cluster nodes. This distribution guarantees fault tolerance and data reliability and enables parallel processing. Since each block is usually duplicated among three nodes, the data can still be recovered from other nodes if one or two nodes fail. Replication strategies like this one are crucial for managing Big Data workloads because they offer high availability and resilience in an environment where hardware failures are frequent. With block sizes usually set to 128 MB or 256 MB, HDFS is also made to manage massive files effectively, reducing the overhead associated with managing many little files.

The fundamental computing architecture of Hadoop, MapReduce, makes it easier to process massive datasets by dividing the work into smaller, more manageable pieces. The Map and Reduce phases are the two primary phases in which the MapReduce system functions. The input data is split into smaller sub-tasks during the Map phase, and each is processed separately to generate key-value pairs. After that, these intermediary key-value pairs are sorted and shuffled to arrange them according to the key. These grouped key-value pairs are combined to create the final output during the Reduce phase. Because of this model's great scalability, Hadoop can effectively handle petabytes of data across thousands of nodes. MapReduce's parallel architecture makes it especially useful for batch processing jobs like data mining, indexing, and large-scale machine learning algorithms.

The resource management layer of Hadoop, known as Yet Another Resource Negotiator (YARN), was included in Hadoop 2.0 to remedy the shortcomings of the original MapReduce framework. With the help of YARN, resource management, and job scheduling are separated from the MapReduce programming paradigm, making Hadoop a more adaptable and effective platform. The architecture of YARN is made up of Node Managers and Resource Managers. While Node Managers operate on each cluster node and oversee the execution of activities on individual nodes, Resource Managers serve as the central authority for allocating resources for applications. Because of the improved resource efficiency and scalability made possible by this division of labor, Hadoop can now support more data processing frameworks than just MapReduce, including Apache Spark and Apache Flink. Hadoop is now a more flexible and potent tool for handling Big Data processing because of YARN's capacity to manage numerous concurrent data processing frameworks.

The amalgamation of HDFS, MapReduce, and YARN creates a sturdy and expandable environment for managing large amounts of data. Extensive dataset management requires distributed storage, which HDFS offers while guaranteeing high availability and fault tolerance. To process big datasets in parallel, MapReduce provides a robust computational paradigm that divides complicated jobs into smaller subtasks that may be handled separately by different cluster members. By managing resources and scheduling jobs, YARN improves the flexibility and efficiency of the Hadoop ecosystem and makes it possible for several data processing frameworks to coexist and run simultaneously.

The Hadoop ecosystem has many more tools and frameworks that enhance its functionality in addition to these fundamental parts. For example, Apache Hive offers a Hadoop-based data warehouse infrastructure that lets users query massive datasets like SQL. This makes utilizing Hadoop's data analysis capabilities simpler for people already familiar with SQL. To make developing MapReduce applications easier, Apache Pig provides a high-level scripting language for data transformation and analytic activities. Running on top of HDFS, Apache HBase is a NoSQL database that offers massive datasets with real-time read/write access. These and other tools like Apache Flume for data intake, Apache Oozie for workflow scheduling, and Apache ZooKeeper for coordination and synchronization comprise a robust ecosystem supporting a wide range of Big Data applications.

Scalability is one of the main advantages of the Hadoop ecosystem. Hadoop's ability to scale out through the addition of more nodes to the cluster allows it to manage growing workloads and data volumes without requiring major modifications to the underlying architecture. The distributed architecture of HDFS and the parallel processing power of MapReduce allow for this scalability. Hadoop is an affordable big data processing option because businesses can add more commodity hardware to increase their clusters as data accumulates.

Fault tolerance is one of Hadoop's main advantages. Data is maintained and accessible even during hardware failures because of HDFS's data replication feature. Because MapReduce provides task-level fault tolerance, unsuccessful tasks can be re-executed on different nodes, guaranteeing that the job can still finish successfully even if one or more individual tasks fail. YARN provides even more fault tolerance by monitoring node health and reallocating resources as required. Hadoop is a dependable platform for mission-critical Big Data applications because of its strong fault tolerance.

The Hadoop environment has advantages, but it also has drawbacks. One of the biggest obstacles is the complexity of operating and sustaining significant Hadoop clusters. Hadoop's distributed architecture necessitates meticulous setup and oversight to guarantee peak efficiency and dependability. Furthermore, Hadoop performs less effectively for interactive queries and real-time data processing than batch processing jobs. Due to this restriction, complementary solutions have emerged, such as Apache Spark, which offers in-memory processing capabilities for quicker data analysis.

Another crucial factor in the Hadoop environment is security. Strong security measures are required to safeguard sensitive data in Hadoop settings due to their distributed and multi-tenant nature. To solve these issues, Hadoop provides a number of security capabilities, such as auditing, encryption, authentication, and authorization. Within the Hadoop ecosystem, two projects called Apache Ranger and Apache Knox improve security by offering perimeter security and centralized security management, respectively.

The Hadoop ecosystem offers a robust and scalable foundation for processing large amounts of data thanks to its essential parts, HDFS, MapReduce, and YARN. While YARN improves resource management and scalability,

MapReduce provides a solid computational model for parallel data processing, while HDFS guarantees dependable and fault-tolerant storage. Combined, these elements create a flexible platform to manage a wide range of Big Data tasks. Even though Hadoop has difficulties with complexity, real-time processing, and security, new developments and related technologies are expanding its capabilities and securing Hadoop's place as a critical component of the Big Data ecosystem. Large volumes of data are still being generated and used by companies. Thus, the Hadoop ecosystem is still crucial for maximizing the potential of Big Data and spurring innovation in various sectors.

Spark and Real-Time Data Processing

Apache Spark has wholly changed the Big Data processing landscape by offering a single analytics engine that is quick and adaptable to handle various data processing jobs. Because of its simplicity of use and capacity for in-memory processing, Spark is a preferred option for engineers and data scientists. This section highlights the importance of Spark Streaming and Kafka for real-time data processing in contemporary data infrastructures while also examining the foundations of Apache Spark.

Fast computation is the goal of the open-source distributed computing system Apache Spark. By providing a more effective data processing paradigm through in-memory computation and a broad range of high-level APIs in Java, Scala, Python, and R, it expands on the MapReduce approach utilized by Hadoop. The Resilient Distributed Dataset (RDD) abstraction, a distributed collection of parallelizable objects, is the central component of Spark. RDDs can be generated from local files, Hadoop Input Formats (such as HDFS files), or pre-existing RDDs that have been altered using functions like reduce, filter, and map. These operations take advantage of Spark's automatic task distribution and fault tolerance management to let users write complicated parallel computations with simplicity.

The performance of Spark is one of its best qualities. Spark eliminates the laborious process of writing intermediate results to disk, a significant bottleneck in conventional MapReduce processing, by retaining data in memory between operations. This means that Spark can be up to 100 times faster in some situations than Hadoop MapReduce. In addition, Spark's DAG (Directed Acyclic Graph) execution engine optimizes the execution plan, guaranteeing effective scheduling of tasks and usage of resources.

Apache Spark performs exceptionally well at real-time data processing via Spark Streaming and batch processing. In addition to the core Spark API, Spark Streaming allows fault-tolerant, high-throughput, and scalable stream processing of real-time data streams. High-level functions like map, reduce, join, and window can be used to express complicated algorithms that analyze data ingested from various sources, including Flume, Kafka, and Kinesis. After processing, the data can be uploaded to databases, file systems, or real-time dashboards.

To process data streams, Spark Streaming divides the input data into micro-batches or batches of pre-defined intervals. Since every micro-batch is handled as an RDD, streaming data may be processed using the same set of Spark operations. Thanks to this micro-batch processing approach, the system can manage large data throughput with the same fault tolerance and scalability as Spark's batch processing. For instance, Spark Streaming may ingest log data from Kafka, aggregate log message counts over sliding windows, and update real-time dashboards with the most recent counts in a log analysis application.

The Apache Software Foundation is currently responsible for maintaining Kafka, a distributed event streaming technology created by LinkedIn that can process billions of events daily. Kafka is a high-throughput, low-latency, fault-tolerant publish-subscribe system that forms the foundation of many real-time data processing pipelines. It separates the producers and consumers of data, enabling flexible and scalable data intake.

Spark Streaming and Kafka integration make for a potent combo for real-time data processing. Kafka streams are an efficient and scalable method of feeding data into Spark Streaming applications. As part of this integration, Kafka is set up as a source for Spark Streaming, where data streams are Kafka topics, and Spark processes them almost instantly. Numerous partitions are possible for each Kafka topic, enabling numerous Spark executors to consume data concurrently and guaranteeing scalability and high throughput.

Establishing a Kafka cluster and generating topics to which data producers (such as web apps, sensors, or logs) submit data are standard steps in the integration process. After that, Spark Streaming uses this data by connecting with the Kafka cluster and reading the messages from the designated topics. Micro-batches of the ingested data are analyzed, and the output can be transmitted to downstream systems for additional analysis or stored back in Kafka, HDFS, or any other storage system.

Applications like fraud detection, recommendation engines, monitoring systems, and analytics depend on real-time processing using Spark Streaming and Kafka. Real-time processing, for example, can follow user activity in e-commerce systems and instantly deliver personalized recommendations. Similarly, real-time fraud detection systems in the financial services industry examine transaction streams to spot questionable activity and sound the alarm before illegal transactions occur.

Fault tolerance is one of the main benefits of combining Spark Streaming with Kafka. Spark and Kafka are both built to handle errors gracefully. Using checkpoints, Spark Streaming enables stream processing applications to bounce back from mistakes without losing data. Conversely, Kafka ensures that data is recovered even if certain brokers fail by replicating messages across several brokers. This combination offers a real-time data processing solution that is highly durable and dependable.

Additionally, due to their scalability, Spark and Kafka are well-suited to handle the ever-increasing volume and velocity of data generated in today's digital environment. Increasing the number of nodes in the cluster can expand both systems. Adding more brokers increases the capability of the Kafka cluster to accommodate more partitions and higher throughput. More executors in Spark enable greater parallelism and quicker micro-batch processing. Because of its scalability, the system may grow with the data and sustain performance levels.

Moreover, Spark and Kafka are surrounded by a vibrant and dynamic environment. To enhance Spark Streaming with Kafka, tools like Apache NiFi and Apache Flink can be used to add further features for data intake, transformation, and real-time processing. For example, Apache Flink provides an alternative stream processing framework with additional features like exactly-once semantics and event-time processing, while Apache NiFi may handle data routing and transformation before feeding it into Kafka.

To summarize, Apache Spark and Spark Streaming, an addon, offer a robust batch and real-time data processing framework. Spark Streaming becomes a potent tool for creating fault-tolerant, high-throughput, and scalable real-time data processing pipelines when paired with Kafka. With the help of this integration, businesses can instantly gain insights from their data, improving their ability to make decisions, react to events as they happen, and create dynamic, data-driven apps. Spark and Kafka will continue to be essential to contemporary data infrastructures as the data landscape changes, fostering efficiency and creativity in various sectors.

CHAPTER IX

Data Science in Practice

Case Studies in Various Industries

Data science—a multidisciplinary subject that combines statistical analysis, machine learning, and data engineering—is revolutionizing several industries by facilitating data-driven innovation and decision-making. This section examines the applications of data science in retail, healthcare, financial, and other industries, emphasizing the significant influence that data science has on these fields.

Data science is revolutionizing medical research and patient care in the healthcare industry. Predictive analytics, personalized care, and operational efficiency have all made significant strides due to the ability to analyze vast amounts of medical data. For instance, predictive analytics can forecast patient outcomes and disease outbreaks using historical data and machine learning algorithms. Hospitals are using predictive models to identify high-risk patients, leading to targeted treatments that enhance patient outcomes and reduce costs. Data science is also instrumental in advancing personalized treatment. By analyzing genetic data and medical records, scientists can tailor medications for each patient, increasing therapeutic effectiveness and reducing side effects. Initiatives like the Precision Medicine Initiative in the United States, which aims to enhance personalized treatment recommendations by integrating genomic data with clinical information, are prime examples of this. Data science is also enhancing operational efficiencies in the healthcare industry. Clinics and hospitals are using data analytics to better allocate resources, streamline administrative processes, reduce wait times, and improve overall patient care.

The finance sector has led the way when using data science to improve consumer experiences, manage risks, and make better decisions. Fraud detection is one of the primary uses of data science in the financial industry. Financial organizations examine transaction patterns and look for anomalies that can point to fraud using machine learning algorithms. Customers are protected, and fraud is prevented thanks to this real-time analysis. Furthermore, data science is crucial in risk assessment and credit rating. To thoroughly evaluate a person's creditworthiness, alternative data sources, including social media activity and transaction history, have been added to traditional credit scoring algorithms. This has made it possible for lenders to extend loans to a broader spectrum of clients and make better-informed decisions. Another area where data science is having a significant impact is algorithmic trading. Financial institutions can exploit market inefficiencies and make substantial profits by evaluating market data and executing trades using intricate algorithms. Additionally, data science is revolutionizing customer service in the financial industry. To increase client happiness and loyalty, banks and other financial institutions use chatbots and AI-driven recommendation systems to offer their customers individualized guidance and support.

Data science is driving innovation in marketing strategies, inventory management, and consumer experience in the retail industry. The use of customized marketing is among the most prominent uses. Retailers use consumer information, like past purchases and browsing patterns, to develop tailored marketing campaigns and recommendations. Offering a more tailored shopping experience boosts consumer loyalty and increases sales. For instance, highly developed recommendation algorithms are used by e-commerce behemoths like Amazon to make product recommendations to users based on their browsing and past buying history. Another crucial area where data science is having an impact is inventory management. Retailers forecast product demand using predictive analytics, which helps them minimize surplus inventory while maintaining the proper stock levels to meet client demands. This lowers expenses and increases operational efficiency. Retailers are also using data science to optimize their pricing tactics. Retailers can use dynamic pricing models to maximize revenue and maintain their competitiveness in the market by studying rival prices, market trends, and customer behavior.

Data science is revolutionizing healthcare, finance, retail, manufacturing, transportation, and entertainment. Data science is applied in manufacturing to optimize production procedures, boost quality assurance, and minimize downtime. For instance, predictive maintenance uses machine learning algorithms to anticipate equipment breakdowns ahead of time, enabling manufacturers to carry out maintenance proactively and avert expensive disruptions. Data on supplier performance, demand trends, and logistical aspects are analyzed by data scientists, which aids manufacturers in streamlining their supply chains. This results in less expensive manufacturing schedules and increased efficiency.

The transportation sector uses data science to increase customer satisfaction, efficiency, and safety. Cities are embracing data analytics in public transportation to optimize schedules and routes depending on traffic patterns and passenger demand. Public transportation networks have become more dependable and effective as a result. Furthermore, data science plays a significant role in how ride-sharing businesses like Uber and Lyft match drivers with passengers, forecast demand, and establish dynamic pricing. Many companies employ real-time data analysis to ensure that their services are effective and sensitive to their clients' needs. Another fascinating use of data science in transportation is autonomous cars. Self-driving cars pave the way for safer and more effective transportation systems using machine-learning algorithms to analyze sensor data and judge navigation and obstacle avoidance in real time.

Data science is also transforming the entertainment sector. Data analytics are used by streaming services such as Netflix and Spotify to suggest material to consumers based on their viewing or listening habits and interests. This tailored strategy boosts subscription retention and maintained user engagement. Data science is also applied in the production of content. Studios and production businesses use audience data to guide their creative strategy and investment decisions by identifying the materials most likely to be successful. Social media platforms utilize data science to assess user engagement and enhance the distribution of information. To maximize engagement and guarantee that users see the most relevant information, algorithms are used to determine which posts show in users' feeds.

Data science is revolutionizing various sectors, including retail, healthcare, banking, and more. Data science is revolutionizing how businesses run and compete by promoting innovation, improving operational efficiencies, and facilitating better-informed decision-making. We may anticipate even more significant changes as the industry develops, resulting in better services, better consumer experiences, and important breakthroughs in technology and business procedures.

Ethical Considerations and Data Privacy

In the era of big data, the paramount importance of data privacy and ethical use cannot be overstated. As data becomes increasingly integrated into the operations of businesses and society, these issues have become critical concerns. This section delves into the moral implications of data usage, examines key laws such as the California Consumer Privacy Act (CCPA) and the General Data Protection Regulation (GDPR), and underscores the imperative of compliance.

Fairness, permission, and openness are the three central tenets of ethical considerations while using data. Informing people about the collection, usage, and sharing of their data is crucial to transparency. Businesses must be transparent about their data practices and give people the knowledge they need to make educated decisions. Since consent gives people control over their data, it is essential to the ethical use of data. Explicit and informed consent ensures that those providing data are aware of the consequences of sharing it and have given their approval voluntarily. Data should not be used to injure or discriminate against certain people or groups to ensure fairness in data utilization. This entails avoiding biased algorithms and ensuring that judgments based on data don't reinforce already-existing disparities or introduce new kinds of prejudice.

The European Union (EU) created the General Data Protection Regulation (GDPR) as a comprehensive legal framework to safeguard EU individuals' personal information and privacy. Since its implementation in May 2018, the GDPR has raised the global bar for privacy and data protection. The GDPR's demand for the lawful, equitable, and transparent handling of personal data is one of its central tenets. Legal justifications for data collection and processing must be established by organizations, such as getting individuals' express consent or meeting contractual requirements. The "right to be forgotten," commonly known as the GDPR, requires people to see their data, correct any inaccuracies, and ask for their information to be deleted. Strict data breach notification requirements are enforced by this rule, which requires enterprises to notify impacted parties as soon as possible of data breaches and report them to regulatory authorities within 72 hours. Serious consequences, including fines of up to €20 million or 4% of the company's yearly global revenue, whichever is higher, may arise from non-compliance with the GDPR. This strict enforcement emphasizes the importance of following moral data standards and safeguarding people's privacy.

Taking effect in January 2020, the California Consumer Privacy Act (CCPA) is another important law designed to improve data privacy. Residents of California are granted many rights regarding their personal information under the CCPA. These rights include the ability to request the deletion of their data and the right to know what personal data is being collected about them and to access it. People also have the option to refuse to have their personal information sold. Businesses must also offer a transparent and easily readable privacy policy and reveal their data collecting and sharing policies by the CCPA. Like the GDPR, the CCPA imposes severe fines for noncompliance, with penalties starting at $2,500 and going up to $7,500 for willful violations. With the CCPA, the US has taken a big step toward increased data privacy, and other governments will be bound to follow suit.

Adherence to data protection laws such as the CCPA and GDPR is legally and morally required. Building trust with stakeholders and customers can be achieved by organizations that place a high priority on data protection and ethical data usage. In a time when data breaches and the improper use of personal information are on the rise, this trust is crucial. Organizations may protect customer information and stop illegal access by putting strong data protection measures, such as encryption, access limits, and frequent security audits. In addition, it is imperative to cultivate a privacy-conscious culture inside a firm. This includes assigning data protection officers to supervise compliance initiatives, creating explicit data governance policies, and educating staff members on data protection principles.

Using cutting-edge technology like machine learning and artificial intelligence (AI) is also subject to ethical problems. Although these technologies have the potential to be very beneficial, they also present specific ethical difficulties. For example, biases in the data that AI algorithms are trained on may unintentionally be perpetuated by the algorithms, producing unjust and discriminatory results. Organizations must implement ethical AI techniques to overcome these obstacles. A few of these practices include guaranteeing diversity in training data, carrying out routine audits to identify and reduce biases, and encouraging openness in algorithmic decision-making.

Furthermore, the ethical use of data depends heavily on data reduction. According to this theory, companies should gather and hold onto the bare minimum of data required for their objectives. Organizations can lower the risk of data breaches and guarantee that they respect people's privacy by following the data reduction guidelines.

The idea of purpose limitation is a crucial component of ethical data usage. According to this principle, information should never be utilized for reasons unrelated to those obtained initially without the individual's consent. Purpose limitation guarantees that people can choose how their information is used and helps prevent data misuse. Organizations also need to be aware of the quality and accuracy of their data. Outdated or inaccurate data can result in erroneous inferences and detrimental decisions. Maintaining the correctness and dependability of data can be aided by routine updating and verification.

Concepts like data privacy and ethical data usage are dynamic; they change as technology develops and society shifts. Data protection policies and procedures must be regularly reviewed and updated as new technologies are developed and data becomes increasingly necessary for daily operations. Maintaining constant communication with stakeholders, such as legislators, consumers, and advocacy organizations, can assist in guaranteeing that data privacy regulations remain applicable and efficient.

In conclusion, ethical data use and privacy are crucial issues in today's data-driven society. Laws like the CCPA and GDPR safeguard people's privacy and ensure data is handled morally. Organizations must abide by these rules to foster trust, protect personal data, and stop data misuse. Organizations may manage the challenges of data ethics and help create a safer and just digital environment by upholding the values of openness, consent, justice, data minimization, and purpose limitation. Sustaining public confidence and protecting the fundamental right to privacy will depend heavily on further efforts to bolster data protection laws and encourage moral data practices.

Building a Data-Driven Culture

It is impossible to overestimate the significance of creating a data-driven culture in the modern company environment. Successful data science integration gives businesses a competitive edge through better decision-making, increased operational effectiveness, and creative product development. To do this, a data science team needs to have a well-defined structure of roles and duties and significant organizational changes. This section outlines the roles and duties crucial for a successful data science team and examines the organizational adjustments required to implement data science.

Organizational perspectives on and uses of data must fundamentally change to become data-driven. Leadership commitment is the first step in this transition. Senior executives need to provide resources to support data initiatives and advocate for the use of data in decision-making processes. Using a top-down approach, the organization is guaranteed to understand the strategic value of data and coordinate its actions accordingly. Leaders must cultivate an atmosphere that promotes data literacy and ongoing education. Critical first stages in this change include funding data-skills training programs for staff members and encouraging a culture of curiosity where data is routinely utilized to challenge presumptions and support choices.

Integrating data science into the primary business operations is another crucial organizational transformation. Organizations should incorporate data scientists into various departments to collaborate closely with business divisions instead of viewing data science as a distinct function. This integration makes better comprehension of domain-specific problems possible, which also guarantees the applicability and usefulness of data-driven solutions. For example, integrating data scientists into marketing departments helps improve customer segmentation and targeting, while having them in operations can minimize inefficiencies and expedite procedures. Cross-functional cooperation between business teams and data scientists promotes creativity and a more comprehensive approach to problem-solving.

Data governance is another essential component of creating a culture driven by data. Strong data governance structures guarantee that the organization's data is correct, standardized, and easily accessible. This entails establishing data ownership, harmonizing data definitions, and putting in place safeguards for data quality. Assuring regulatory compliance and advancing best practices in data management, a Chief Data Officer (CDO) or a position akin to it should manage data governance initiatives. Good data governance encourages employees to use data in their daily duties by enhancing data reliability and fostering trust in its utilization.

A well-organized data science team with distinct roles and duties is the foundation of any data-driven company. A productive data science team usually consists of specialized positions, each bringing different knowledge and abilities. The leading positions in a data science team are data scientists, data engineers, machine learning engineers, data analysts, and business analysts.

Data scientists are the leading designers of data-driven solutions. They know about machine learning algorithms, statistical techniques, and programming languages like R and Python. Data scientists are responsible for investigating databases, creating predictive models, and producing insights that inform business choices. Their work frequently includes speculating, testing, and iterating to develop reliable models to resolve challenging business issues.

Conversely, data engineers concentrate on the architecture and infrastructure to enable data science activities. They are adept at creating and managing data pipelines, guaranteeing effective data collection, archiving, and processing. Data engineers are experts in tools and technologies like Hadoop, Spark, and SQL and deal with large-scale distributed systems. Their involvement is essential to guaranteeing that data scientists have access to the clean, well-organized data required for their analysis.

Machine learning engineers fill the gap between software engineering and data science. They are in charge of using machine learning models and ensuring they function at a large scale. Their tasks include creating APIs, integrating models with current systems, and optimizing algorithms. Their ability to develop scalable and dependable machine learning systems stems from their proficiency with both data science and software engineering concepts.

Data analysts are essential for understanding data and producing insights that can be put into practice. They know how to use data visualization programs like Tableau, Power BI, and Excel and how to use SQL to query databases. They work to find patterns, trends, and anomalies in data so that business units can have the knowledge they need to make wise decisions. They frequently collaborate closely with business analysts to convert data discoveries into recommendations for strategy.

The business stakeholders and the data science team are connected through business analysts. They are in charge of converting business requirements into data-driven solutions and thoroughly understand the business domain. Business analysts collaborate with data scientists to ensure the models and analyses support organizational objectives. Additionally, they ensure that non-technical stakeholders understand and can effectively implement data-driven decisions by sharing insights and recommendations.

Promoting cooperation and communication inside the data science team and throughout the company is another necessary step in creating a culture driven by data. Frequent gatherings for brainstorming, workshops, and meetings can ensure that everyone agrees with the organization's data strategy and to share information. Innovation and constant development depend on fostering a collaborative atmosphere where team members can openly exchange ideas and criticism.

Organizations also need to invest in the appropriate tools and technologies to support data science activities. This comprises cloud-based infrastructure for scalable data processing, data visualization tools, and sophisticated analytics platforms. Effective data-driven solutions must be developed by giving data scientists the tools they need to explore and innovate.

To sum up, creating a data-driven culture necessitates major organizational adjustments and a clear assignment of duties within a data science team. Essential elements of this transition include strong data governance, promoting data literacy, integrating data science into fundamental business processes, and demonstrating leadership commitment. Data scientists, data engineers, machine learning engineers, data analysts, and business analysts are just a few jobs necessary for a successful data science team since each brings exceptional knowledge and abilities. By promoting cooperation, strategic tool investment, and integrating data science into the organizational framework, organizations may fully leverage data to stimulate innovation, enhance decision-making, and accomplish strategic objectives. The significance of developing a data-centric attitude and a data science-embracing culture will only increase as organizations continue to change in this data-driven era, setting them up for long-term success and market competitiveness.

CHAPTER X

Future Trends in Data Science and Analytics

Emerging Technologies

Thanks to developments in artificial intelligence (AI), machine learning, and upcoming technologies like quantum computing, the discipline of data science and analytics is expanding quickly. These developments can significantly improve data analysis capabilities, empowering businesses to gain a deeper understanding, produce more precise forecasts, and resolve ever-more complicated issues. This section examines the future directions of data science and analytics, with particular attention paid to developments in AI and machine learning and the possible influence of quantum computing in this field.

AI and machine learning have entirely changed the data science field by automating data processing, enabling predictive analytics, and revealing patterns previously buried in enormous datasets. These technologies are anticipated to advance further and become essential to data science in the future. Creating more sophisticated neural networks and intense learning models is one of the significant developments in artificial intelligence and machine learning. With previously unheard-of precision, these models can interpret massive volumes of unstructured data, including pictures, videos, and spoken language. Deep learning algorithms will be more accurate and dependable when they take on increasingly challenging tasks, such as autonomous driving and real-time language translation.

Another noteworthy trend is the growing application of reinforcement learning, a machine learning in which an agent learns to make decisions by interacting with its environment and receiving feedback. There is a lot of promise for reinforcement learning in fields like robotics, gaming, and finance. It can be applied to data science to enhance decision-making, optimize workflows, and create intelligent systems that adjust to changing circumstances. Reinforcement learning techniques, for instance, can be used to manage dynamic pricing schemes, improve personalized suggestions in real-time, and optimize supply chain processes.

Another new movement that tackles the opaque nature of many AI models is explainable AI (XAI). An increasing number of crucial sectors, like healthcare, banking, and criminal justice, are utilizing AI systems, and as a result, their decision-making processes must be more transparent and accountable. Explainable AI aims to improve human comprehension and interpretation of AI models. To boost user confidence in AI systems, methods must be developed to let people observe how a model makes a given choice. XAI will be essential for ethical AI use, regulatory compliance, and broader adoption of AI technology.

Quantum computing, in addition to developments in AI and machine learning, has the potential to transform data science and analytics completely. Using the ideas of quantum mechanics, quantum computers can execute calculations tenfold quicker than on a conventional computer. This skill will significantly impact data science, especially when it comes to solving issues that traditional computers are currently unable to handle. Numerous facets of data science, including simulation, encryption analysis, and optimization, can benefit from quantum computing.

The optimization domain is among data science's most promising quantum computing uses. Finding the optimal answer from a large pool of possibilities is common in real-world issues, including drug development, supply chain management, and financial portfolio optimization. The combinatorial proliferation of options makes these tasks difficult for classical computers. However, the time needed to determine the best answer can be drastically decreased because quantum computers can assess numerous alternatives simultaneously. This potential can result in important discoveries in fields where optimization plays a significant role.

Machine learning techniques could be improved by quantum computing as well. A new field called quantum machine learning (QML) combines machine learning methods with quantum computers. Larger datasets can be handled using QML algorithms, speeding up the training process for complicated models and increasing prediction accuracy. For example, support vector machines and neural networks may execute faster and more accurately in quantum than in classical equivalents. QML can potentially be a vital tool for data scientists as quantum hardware advances, allowing them to address issues currently outside the purview of traditional machine learning.

Cryptographic analysis is another field where quantum computing may significantly impact. Because quantum computers can solve discrete logarithms and integer factorization problems quickly, they can break many of the cryptographic schemes currently used to encrypt data, including RSA and ECC. This hampers data security but also motivates the creation of cryptographic methods immune to quantum errors. To ensure data security in the future, cryptographers and data scientists are developing new encryption techniques that can fend off quantum attacks.

New frameworks and tools that bridge the gap between quantum and classical computing are also necessary for integrating quantum computing into data science. Shortly, hybrid quantum-classical algorithms—which incorporate the best features of both computer paradigms—will probably be quite significant. These algorithms use quantum computers for the most computationally demanding portions while using classical computers for data preprocessing and other tasks that do not require quantum speedups. This method can increase processing efficiency and improve data scientists' access to quantum computing.

The convergence of AI, machine learning, and quantum computing will influence the direction of data science and analytics. To keep up with the latest technology developments, organizations must invest in the necessary infrastructure, hire new employees, and promote an innovative culture. Data scientists, who must thoroughly understand classical and quantum computing approaches, will be essential to this shift.

Furthermore, as these technologies advance, ethical considerations will always come first. For AI and machine learning to be widely used, it will be essential to guarantee that the models are impartial, open, and responsible. In a post-quantum era, creating cryptographic techniques resistant to quantum entanglement will safeguard data security and privacy.

In conclusion, substantial developments in AI and machine learning, along with the revolutionary potential of quantum computing, will define future data science and analytics trends. These technologies promise to improve data analysis capabilities, allowing firms to solve complex problems more quickly, get deeper insights, and make more accurate predictions. Data science will change due to the combination of these technologies as AI models get more complex and explicable and as quantum computing develops. To fully utilize data science and analytics in the upcoming years, organizations that adopt these trends and invest in developing the requisite infrastructure and personnel will be in a strong position. As these developments occur, upholding moral principles and guaranteeing data security will be essential to building confidence and making long-term progress.

The Role of Automation and AI

Automation and artificial intelligence (AI) have become critical drivers of efficiency and innovation in the quickly changing technology field. Artificial intelligence (AI) has many uses, but two that stand out for their revolutionary potential are automated machine learning (AutoML) and AI-driven decision-making systems. These developments are changing how firms run, increasing efficiency, and opening the door to better, more informed decision-making. This section examines the function of AI and AutoML-driven decision-making systems and their advantages, disadvantages, and potential future effects on various businesses.

Automated machine learning, or AutoML, is a significant advancement in data science. In the past, developing machine learning models needed significant proficiency in data preprocessing, model selection, hyperparameter tuning, and statistics. This laborious process was frequently only available to highly qualified data scientists. Many intricate and time-consuming tasks can be automated using autoML, which democratizes machine learning. It makes these potent technologies more accessible by enabling non-experts to build and use machine learning models with little assistance.

AutoML functions by automating every step of a machine learning project's workflow, from selecting and optimizing models to preparing data. It is first cleaned and processed to make the data appropriate for analysis. After that, autoML systems investigate many techniques and hyperparameters to determine which model is optimal for the current task. Methods like hyperparameter optimization, model selection, and automated feature engineering are used to improve model performance. In addition to quickening the creation of machine learning models, this technique frequently produces models that are more reliable and accurate than those created by hand by human specialists.

There are numerous advantages to AutoML. First, it speeds up the implementation of AI solutions by drastically reducing the time and effort needed to create machine learning models. This is especially helpful in finance, healthcare, and retail sectors, where making decisions quickly is essential. Second, by freeing data scientists from the mundane chore of developing new models, AutoML improves productivity by enabling them to concentrate on more strategic and challenging projects. Furthermore, AutoML encourages a culture of data-driven business decision-making by making machine learning understandable to non-experts, allowing a larger spectrum of staff members to use AI in their workflows.

Another crucial use of artificial intelligence is in AI-driven decision-making systems. These systems help businesses make more precise, timely, and informed decisions. They use cutting-edge algorithms to sift through massive amounts of data, spot trends, and produce insights that can direct tactical decisions. When AI is included in decision-making processes, decision quality is increased overall, efficiency is increased, and human bias is decreased.

The capacity of AI-driven decision-making systems to process and evaluate enormous volumes of data in real time is one of its main advantages. AI can monitor market conditions, assess investment portfolios, and make suggestions for maximizing returns in industries such as finance. AI-driven healthcare systems can forecast disease outbreaks, assess patient data, and provide individualized treatment regimens. Organizations are better equipped to take advantage of new possibilities, adapt quickly to changing circumstances, and successfully manage risks with access to real-time data.

AI-driven decision-making systems also perform exceptionally well at spotting intricate connections and patterns that human analysts might miss. AI, for example, can be used in marketing to evaluate consumer behavior data and find trends and preferences. This helps companies better target their marketing efforts and increase customer engagement. Artificial intelligence (AI) in manufacturing can forecast equipment breakdowns and improve maintenance plans, saving downtime and increasing operational effectiveness. Artificial intelligence (AI)-driven systems facilitate better comprehension of diverse phenomena and more informed decision-making by revealing hidden insights.

Adopting AI and AutoML-driven decision-making systems is challenging, though. The issue of interpretability and transparency is one of the main worries. Many AI models function as "black boxes," making comprehending how they arrive at their findings challenging. This is especially true with deep learning-based models. This lack of transparency can be problematic in industries like healthcare and banking, where explainability is essential. Building trust and maintaining regulatory compliance require AI systems to have transparent, understandable decision-making processes.

Data security and privacy are also major issues. AI-driven systems need large volumes of data, which may be private or sensitive. It is crucial to keep sensitive data safe from breaches and ensure data protection laws are followed. Organizations must set up explicit data governance frameworks to protect data integrity and privacy and put strong security measures in place.

Potential bias in AI models is another problem. The resulting AI systems may reinforce or even worsen biases present in the training data for these models. Unfair or discriminatory results may result from this, especially in the recruiting, lending, and law enforcement sectors. To address AI bias, fairness-aware algorithm development, diversity, and data quality must all be carefully considered. The future of AI- and AutoML-driven decision-making systems is bright, notwithstanding these obstacles. Technological developments in explainable AI (XAI) are improving the interpretability of AI models, facilitating a better understanding and confidence in their conclusions. Scientists are working on methods to shed light on the workings of AI models and identify the variables that affect their forecasts. These developments will be essential for the broader application of AI in fields where openness is critical.

Advancements in federated learning and differential privacy also enhance data security and privacy. Through federated learning, privacy can be maintained by training

AI models on decentralized data sources without requiring the sharing of raw data. Differential privacy techniques allow for accurate analysis while maintaining individual privacy protection by adding noise to the data. Some of the main issues surrounding the adoption of AI are being addressed by these innovations.

In summary, data science and organizational operations are changing due to the influence of automation and artificial intelligence (AI) in the form of AutoML and AI-driven decision-making systems. By automating complex processes and making it possible for non-experts to create and implement models, autoML democratizes access to machine learning. Artificial intelligence (AI)-powered decision-making systems analyze vast amounts of data and find hidden patterns to improve the effectiveness and quality of judgments. Even if issues like bias, data privacy, and transparency still need to be resolved, continuous progress opens the door to more reliable and robust AI solutions. Organizations that continue to use these technologies will have a significant competitive advantage that will spur efficiency and innovation in various sectors. Data science and AI have a bright future, full of fascinating developments and game-changing effects

The Future Landscape

Data science and analytics are expected to undergo significant change during the next ten years due to technological breakthroughs, the growing significance of data in decision-making, and the changing responsibilities of data scientists and analysts. The increasing recognition of data's value by firms across various industries is anticipated to drive the need for proficient specialists in this domain, thereby expanding the range and intricacy of their duties. This section looks at the state of data science in the next ten years, projecting significant developments and analyzing the changing roles of analysts and data scientists.

One of the most important forecasts for data science's future is that machine learning (ML) and artificial intelligence (AI) will continue to grow. These technologies, which automate complex operations, improve predictive skills, and extract insights from enormous datasets, are expected to become increasingly crucial to data analytics. We may anticipate more advanced AI and ML over the next ten years as deep learning, reinforcement learning, and natural language processing developments produce more precise and valuable insights. Because of this progress, data scientists and analysts will need to gain a deeper grasp of how to utilize these technologies to solve real-world problems and stay up to date on the newest algorithms and approaches.

The growing significance of big data and the Internet of Things (IoT) is another significant development. Data scientists and analysts must create new techniques for organizing, processing, and interpreting the massive amounts of data connected devices produce. Considerable data handling skills will be essential, necessitating knowledge of cloud computing platforms and distributed computing frameworks like Hadoop and Spark. IoT data integration with traditional datasets will provide hurdles in terms of data integration, storage, and privacy, but it will also open up new avenues for insights. To successfully integrate and analyze data from many sources, data experts will be essential in resolving these issues.

Data security and privacy will continue to be top priorities in data science. Protecting sensitive and personal data from breaches and ensuring it complies with changing standards will be essential given the volume of collected personal and sensitive data. Data scientists and analysts must learn much about ethical issues and data governance during the next ten years. They will handle complicated regulatory situations, put strong security measures in place, and ensure data is handled appropriately. This will entail keeping up with recent developments in data protection legislation, including the California Consumer Privacy Act (CCPA) and the General Data Protection Regulation (GDPR), and creating plans to assure compliance.

It is also anticipated that data scientists' and analysts' roles will grow more multidisciplinary. These specialists must work closely with other departments, such as marketing, finance, operations, and human resources, as data becomes an increasingly important component of corporate strategy. Thanks to this cross-functional cooperation, organizations will be able to use data more effectively and spur innovation throughout the whole company. Data scientists and analysts will require a thorough understanding of the business domains they assist in addition to good communication and teamwork abilities. They will serve as a point of contact for stakeholders with and without technical backgrounds, converting intricate data insights into workable business plans.

Furthermore, the democratization of data science methods and technologies will only accelerate. Thanks to automated machine learning (AutoML) developments and intuitive analytics systems, even non-experts can conduct complex data analysis. This democratization will not diminish the function of data scientists and analysts; instead, it will cause them to concentrate on more intricate and strategic projects. They will supervise the application of these instruments, guaranteeing the caliber and precision of the analyses and offering advice on optimal procedures. Organizations may cultivate a more data-driven culture by enabling and mentoring a wider variety of employees to interact with data, with data scientists and analysts playing a pivotal role.

Ethics and bias are another crucial area of study in AI and data science. It will be essential to ensure AI systems are impartial, open, and fair as they become more commonplace. It will be necessary for data scientists and analysts to become knowledgeable in ethical AI, recognize potential sources of bias in data and algorithms, and put mitigation strategies in place. This will entail creating algorithms that consider fairness, auditing AI systems regularly, and encouraging openness in the model decision-making process. It will be necessary for data professionals to participate in broader conversations about the effects of artificial intelligence on society to address ethical problems, which will provide both a technological and societal challenge.

Future data scientists' and analysts' education and training will likewise change to fulfill these new objectives. It will be necessary for traditional educational programs to modify their curricula to include new technology and multidisciplinary methods. Professionals must stay current with the latest advancements in data science, artificial intelligence, and related sectors, making continuous learning imperative. Professional certifications, boot camps, and online courses will all be essential for continuing education and skill development. Companies must also spend money on training and development programs to guarantee that their data teams stay at the forefront of their industry.

The idea of integrating quantum computing into data science is exciting in terms of technological improvements. Data processing could undergo a revolution thanks to quantum computing, which can execute intricate computations at previously unheard-of rates. Although technology is still in its infancy, quantum computing has the potential to significantly improve the skills of data scientists and analysts by allowing them to solve problems that are currently unsolvable for conventional computers. Quantum algorithms for machine learning, optimization, and data analysis might be developed during the next ten years, expanding the field of data science.

In conclusion, data science and analytics will see tremendous breakthroughs and transformations during the next ten years. Data scientists and analysts' responsibilities will change with time, becoming more multidisciplinary, team-oriented, and ethically conscious. These professionals must keep up with the latest advancements in AI, machine learning, and big data technologies, acquire new skills, and adjust to shifting market demands. Incorporating quantum computing will shape the future of data science, the democratization of data science tools, and the focus on data security and privacy. Data scientists and analysts will be essential in promoting innovation, enhancing decision-making, and adding value for businesses in all sectors by embracing these trends and challenges. Data science is expected to undergo a tremendous transition shortly, with countless chances for individuals skilled in navigating this dynamic and quickly changing sector.

CONCLUSION

"Data Science and Analytics Essentials: The Revolution of Decision-Making: Leveraging Data in the Digital Age" provides a comprehensive exploration of the transformative power of data in contemporary business and society. This book underscores how data science and analytics revolutionize decision-making processes, enabling organizations to harness the vast amounts of data generated in the digital age. Delving into the core principles, methodologies, and technologies equips readers with a deep understanding of effectively leveraging data for strategic advantage.

The journey through this book is not just a theoretical exploration. It highlights the critical role of data-driven insights in driving real-world innovation, improving operational efficiency, and enhancing customer experiences. It also emphasizes the practical importance of building a data-centric culture within organizations, where data literacy and ethical considerations are prioritized, making the book's content immediately applicable in the reader's professional life.

This book serves as both a foundational guide and a forward-looking resource for professionals, students, and enthusiasts. It encourages embracing the opportunities and challenges the digital age presents, fostering a mindset of continuous learning and adaptation. As data continues to shape the world, the insights and knowledge from this book will empower readers to navigate and thrive in the revolution of decision-making.

Thank you for buying and reading/ listening to our book. If you found this book useful/ helpful please take a few minutes and leave a review on the platform where you purchased our book. Your feedback matters greatly to us.

* 9 7 9 8 3 3 0 2 3 2 0 0 0 *